■ ■ ■

The PSYCHEDELIC JOURNEY
of MARLENE DOBKIN DE RIOS

"This book describes the life and work of one of anthropology's premier border-crossers. Marlene Dobkin de Rios was one of the first to postulate that hallucinogenic substances played an integral part in the development of many aspects of human culture and has clearly and forcefully distinguished between the constructive and the destructive uses of these substances. She has built bridges between anthropology and psychology, theory and practice, and traditional and modern cultures. Over the course of her adventurous life, she has learned love magic from women concerned about her then single status, used fortune-telling cards as an ethnographic research method, and counseled burn victims and other traumatized individuals using insights gleaned from her studies of shamanism. A fascinating book about a fascinating individual."

JOHN R. BAKER, PH.D., PROFESSOR OF ANTHROPOLOGY,
MOORPARK COLLEGE, AND COAUTHOR OF *SUPERNATURAL
AS NATURAL: A BIOCULTURAL APPROACH TO RELIGION*

"Dobkin de Rios is one of the few professional anthropologists who has had the courage to describe her personal experiences with psychedelics. Hers is a compelling story about how direct experience resulted in both wisdom and discernment."

JOHN W. HOOPES, DIRECTOR OF GLOBAL INDIGENOUS
NATIONS STUDIES PROGRAM AND ASSOCIATE PROFESSOR
OF ANTHROPOLOGY, UNIVERSITY OF KANSAS

The PSYCHEDELIC JOURNEY of MARLENE DOBKIN DE RIOS

45 YEARS WITH SHAMANS, AYAHUASQUEROS, AND ETHNOBOTANISTS

MARLENE DOBKIN DE RIOS, PH.D.

Park Street Press
Rochester, Vermont • Toronto, Canada

Park Street Press
One Park Street
Rochester, Vermont 05767
www.ParkStPress.com

Park Street Press is a division of Inner Traditions International

Library of Congress Cataloging-in-Publication Data
Dobkin de Rios, Marlene.
  The psychedelic journey of Marlene Dobkin de Rios : 45 years with shamans,
ayahuasqueros, and ethnobotanists / Marlene Dobkin de Rios, Ph.D.
      p. cm.
  Includes bibliographical references and index.
  Summary: "A look inside almost half a century of pioneering research in the Amazon
and Peru by a noted anthropologist studying hallucinogens, including ayahuasca"—
Provided by publisher.
  ISBN 978-1-59477-313-6
  1. Dobkin de Rios, Marlene. 2. Women anthropologists—Peru—Iquitos—Biography.
3. Women ethnobotanists—Peru—Iquitos Region—Biography. 4. Shamanism—
Peru—Iquitos Region. 5. Healing—Peru—Iquitos Region. 6. Hallucinogenic plants—
Peru—Iquitos Region. 7. Hallucinogenic drugs and religious experience—Peru—Iquitos
Region. 8. Ayahuasca ceremony—Peru—Iquitos Region. 9. Ayahuasca—Therapeutic
use—Peru—Iquitos Region. 10. Banisteriopsis—Therapeutic use—Peru—Iquitos
Region. 11. Iquitos Region (Peru)—Social life and customs. I. Title.
  GN21.D63A3 2009
  301.092—dc22

                                                                                          2009021951

Printed and bound in the United States by Lake Book Manufacturing

10   9   8   7   6   5   4   3   2   1

Text design and layout by Virginia Scott Bowman
This book was typeset in Garamond Premier Pro with Arno Pro, Agenda, and
Schneidler Initials as display typefaces

To send correspondence to the author of this book, mail a first-class letter to the author
c/o Inner Traditions • Bear & Company, One Park Street, Rochester, VT 05767, and
we will forward the communication. The author also may be contacted at her website:
www.marlenedobkinderios.com.

Contents

Foreword

ON EARTH, THERE ARE SOME eight hundred thousand species of plants feeding on the light of the sun. Of these, only a few thousand yield food and medicine, and only a mere hundred or so contain the compounds that transport the mind to distant realms of ethereal wonder. Strictly speaking, a hallucinogen is any chemical substance that distorts the senses and produces hallucinations—perceptions or experiences that depart dramatically from ordinary reality. Academics have called these drugs psychotomimetics (psychosis mimickers), psychotaraxics (mind disturbers), and psychedelics (mind manifesters). These dry-sounding terms quite inadequately describe the remarkable effects the compounds have on the human mind. Indeed, the sensations are so unearthly, the visions so startling, that most hallucinogenic plants acquired a revered place in indigenous cultures. In rare cases they were even worshipped as gods incarnate. Some scholars, in fact, prefer the term *entheogen,* suggesting a pharmacological capacity "to reveal the god within." For Marlene Dobkin de Rios, who has dedicated her career as an anthropologist and ethnobotanist to the study of these remarkable plants, they are simply sacred medicines, for this indeed is what they embody for the Indian peoples who understand them best.

In the worldwide distribution of hallucinogenic plants, there is a remarkable anomaly that illustrates something fundamental about the role these plants play in traditional societies. Of the 120 or more such plants found to date, well over 100 are native to the Americas; the rest of the world has contributed fewer than twenty. In part, this uneven distribution is a reflection of the emphasis of academic research. A good many of these plants were first documented by the legendary Amazonian plant explorer and the father of modern ethnobotany, Richard Evans Schultes, and his students, at the Harvard Botanical Museum and elsewhere. Marlene Dobkin de Rios was among the many remarkable young scholars who fell under his spell.

This cadre, led by the great professor, did much of its research in the Americas. Still, if hallucinogenic plants had been a dominant feature of traditional cultures in Eurasia, Africa, Australia, and Polynesia, surely they would have shown up in the extensive ethnographic literature and in the journals of traders and missionaries. With few notable exceptions, they do not. Nor is this discrepancy due to floristic peculiarities. The rain forests of West Africa and Southeast Asia, in particular, are exceedingly rich and diverse. Moreover, the peoples of these regions have most successfully explored them for biodynamic compounds for use both as medicines and poisons. In fact, as much as any other material trait, the manipulation of toxic plants is a consistent theme throughout sub-Saharan African societies.

The Amerindians, for their part, were certainly no strangers to plant toxins. They commonly exploited them as arrow and dart poisons. Yet while the peoples of Africa consistently used these toxic preparations on one another, the Amerindians almost never did. And whereas the Amerindians successfully explored their forests for hallucinogens, the Africans did not. The use of any pharmacologically active plant is firmly rooted in culture. So if the African peoples did not exploit their forests for psychoactive drugs, it is because they had no cultural need or desire to do so. They had, through spirit possession and trance, another avenue to the divine. In the Americas, by contrast, the use of plant hallucinogens lies at the very heart of traditional life: it is the essence of the shamanic art of healing.

In Amerindian societies, disease is not defined by the presence of pathogens alone, but rather as a state of imbalance or disequilibrium that must be addressed on multiple levels. Illnesses may be treated symptomatically much as we do in allopathic medicine, yet in place of medicinal drugs tribal peoples employ medicinal plants, many of which are indeed pharmacologically active and are sources of many of the drugs in a modern pharmacy. But critically this level of treatment is deemed to be mundane by native healers: to really get to the source of the sickness or misfortune, the shaman must invoke some state of ecstasy. Soaring away on the wings of trance to reach the metaphysical realm, he or she can work deeds of medical, magical, and mystical rescue. This accounts for the role of the sacred plants, these medicines of the mind.

Scholars such as Marlene Dobkin de Rios are interested in these plants not simply because of their dazzling pharmacological effects but also for what they can tell us about a different way of knowing. Consider the most legendary of all shamanic medicines of the Northwest Amazon, ayahuasca, or yagé, the vine of the soul. This is not a single plant but a preparation, a combination of plants. The fundamental ingredient is the inner bark of a woody liana, *Banisteriopsis caapi,* often itself referred to as ayahuasca. The active compounds are the beta-carbolines harmine and harmaline, whose subjective effects—enabling people under the influence to experience various forms of telepathy—are suggested by the fact that when first isolated they were known as telepathine. Taken alone, an infusion of the plant induces subtle visions, blues and purples, slow undulating waves of color.

Long ago, however, the shamans of the Northwest Amazon discovered that the effects could be dramatically enhanced by the addition of a number of subsidiary plants. This practice is an important feature of many folk preparations, and it stems, in part, from the fact that different chemical compounds in relatively small concentrations may effectively potentiate one another. Two of these admixtures are of particular interest: *Psychotria viridis,* a shrub in the coffee family, and *Diplopterys cabrerana,* a forest liana closely related to ayahuasca.

Unlike ayahuasca, both these plants contain tryptamines, powerful psychoactive compounds that when smoked or snuffed induce a very rapid, brief, and intense intoxication marked by astonishing visual imagery. Taken orally, however, these potent compounds have no effect because they are denatured by an enzyme, monoamine oxidase (MAO), found in the human gut. Tryptamines can be taken orally only if combined with an MAO inhibitor.

Amazingly, the beta-carbolines found in ayahuasca are inhibitors of precisely this sort. Thus when ayahuasca is combined with either one of these plants, the result is a synergistic effect, a biochemical version of the whole being greater than the sum of the parts. The visions, as the Amazonian Indians say, become brighter, and the blue and purple hues are augmented by the full spectrum of the rainbow.

When I first witnessed and experienced this remarkable example of shamanic alchemy, what astonished me was not so much the raw effects of the medicine— stunning as they were—as the intellectual process underlying the creation of these complex preparations. The Amazonian flora contains perhaps eighty thousand species of vascular plants alone. How did the Indians learn to identify and combine, in such a sophisticated manner, these morphologically dissimilar plants with such unique and complementary chemical properties? The standard scientific explanation, trial and error, may well account for certain innovations; but at another level it is but a euphemism disguising the fact that ethnobotanists really have no idea how Indians originally made their discoveries.

The problem with trial and error is that the elaboration of the preparations often involves procedures that are exceedingly complex or that yield products of little or no obvious or immediate value. *Banisteriopsis caapi* is an inedible, nondescript liana that seldom flowers. True, its bark is bitter, but scarcely more so than a hundred other forest vines. An infusion of the bark causes vomiting and severe diarrhea, hardly conditions that would encourage further experimentation. Yet not only did the Indians persist, but they became so deft at manipulating the various ingredients that they developed dozens of recipes, each yielding potions of various strengths and nuances for specific ceremonial and ritual purposes.

The Indians have their own explanations—rich cosmological accounts that from their perspective are inherently logical: sacred plants that journeyed up the Milk River in the belly of an anaconda; potions created by the primordial jaguar; the drifting souls of shamans dead from the beginning of time. As scientists we are taught not to take these myths literally. But the stories do suggest a certain delicate balance, the thoughts of a people who do not distinguish between the supernatural and the mundane. The Indians believe in the power of plants, accept the existence of magic, and acknowledge the potency of the spirit. Magical and mystical ideas enter the very texture of their thinking. Their botanical knowledge cannot be separated from their metaphysics.

When in the 1940s Richard Evans Schultes lived among the Ingano of the upper Putumayo, in Colombia, he noted that the shamans recognized seven kinds of ayahuasca liana, all of which to his Harvard-trained taxonomic eye referred to the same species. Among the Siona-Secoya in eastern Ecuador, he documented eighteen varieties, which were distinguished on the basis of the strength and the color of the visions they produced, the trading history of the plant, the authority and lineage of the shaman, even the tone and key of the plants' incantations when taken on the night of a full moon. Schultes used to joke with his students that such a system of classification would not earn you a degree in botany at Harvard. But, he would add with a smile, it was a methodology that was much more interesting than the standard scientific technique of counting flower parts!

This approach also suggested the possibility of a completely different way of knowing—the infinite intellectual possibilities of a mind unshackled and free of the constraints of Western logic and reason. This was not to say for an instant that the peoples of the forest were incapable of rational thought. To the contrary, Schultes always considered the shamans to be natural philosophers, utterly devoted to experimentation and the power of empirical observation. He simply suggested that theirs was another way of thinking and being, of orienting their intuitions in social and spiritual space.

This, more than anything, was the quality of the man that drew into his orbit such an astonishing congregation of scholars and seekers in the late 1960s. His students ranged from quietly conservative, earnest botanists to a somewhat more unusual group drawn to his pioneering work on hallucinogens. Among his many acolytes was Marlene Dobkin de Rios. I, too, was a student of Schultes, and because I was a bit younger, hers was a name that I first encountered in scientific papers. I was enchanted by her accounts, many of which are remembered in this book. Wherever I alighted it seemed that she had already been there, and her papers were lodestars, guiding my way.

This said, until I read this memoir I had no idea what she had gone through, or the depth to which she had devoted herself to her quest. Truth be told, most of us who were drawn to the study of these astonishing plants were in it because we were seeking personal transformation. This was not something to advertise in the academy. But without doubt it motivated us all. Marlene's account is refreshingly honest about all of this. She was a serious scholar, but also a seeker.

⁂

When we look back on the extraordinary changes that have taken place over the past fifty years, what do we see? People of color—that horrible term—have gone from the woodshed to the White House; women have moved from the kitchen to the boardroom; gay men and women have gone from the closet to the altar. Fifty years ago, just getting people to stop throwing trash out of a car window was considered a great environmental victory. No one spoke of the biosphere or biodiversity, terms that today are part of the vocabulary of schoolchildren. Rachel Carson was a lone voice in the wild. The poet Gary Snyder, the prophet of the deep-ecology movement, once told me that in the 1950s he would hitchhike across the country simply to have dinner with someone whom he could relate to. No one spoke of our capacity to transform the atmosphere.

The vision of Earth from space would not come to us until

Christmas Eve 1968, when *Apollo 8* first went around the dark side of the moon. Today the entire world is bound together as a consequence of that image, even as the miracle of the Internet has spread like a mycelium, bypassing traditional mechanisms of communication, liberating everyone so as to take their place around a global campfire that has become the symbol of freedom for the entire world.

What I find odd, and what I think Marlene is at least implicitly suggesting with her decision to write this memoir at this time, is that when we consider all the ingredients in this historic recipe of social change that has taken place over the past half century, there is one contribution that is consistently expunged from the record: that of the untold millions of men and women, old and young, who willingly and with delight have lain prostrate before the gates of awe, having taken one of these remarkable magical plants.

The opposition warned of dire consequences, insisting that these substances could irrevocably and permanently alter the mind and body of anyone exposed to them. What these people in their fear failed to understand was that this was precisely the point: we wanted to be transformed. Not only did I take these plants, but I enjoyed the experience immensely. There is no part of my being that was not affected by the experience. I do not believe that I would write the way I do, think as I think, and understand as a scholar such fundamental notions as cultural relativism had I not had endured with glee the soul-shattering experience that these plants induced. For me, as I suspect for Marlene Dobkin de Rios, these experiences were gifts from the divine, sacred messages that reminded those of us who live in a world stripped of the sacred that we, too, have the right to dream.

WADE DAVIS

Wade Davis holds degrees in anthropology and biology and received his Ph.D. in ethnobotany from Harvard University. He spent more than three years in the Amazon and Andes as a plant explorer, ethnobotanist, and photographer, living among fifteen tribal groups in eight Latin American nations while making some six thousand botanical collections. Presently a research associate of the Instituto Caribe de Antropologia y Sociologia in Caracas, Venezuela, he is an honorary research associate of the Institute of Economic Botany of the New York Botanical Garden, a collaborator in botany at the National Museum of Natural History of the Smithsonian Institution, adjunct professor in the department of biology at Southern Illinois University-Carbondale, research associate of the department of anthropology at the University of British Columbia, a Fellow of the Linnean Society, and the executive director of the Endangered People's Project. Since 1994 Davis has served as vice president for Ethnobotany and Conservation at Andes Pharmaceuticals, Inc., a development-stage biotech company engaged in biodiversity prospecting in the Andes and the Amazon region of South America. He is the author of many scientific articles and books and lectures around the world on a broad array of scientific topics.

Introduction

IT WAS THREE O'CLOCK IN the afternoon as our group of friends left the pickup to visit the Anaconda Center in Iquitos, Peru, on the famous shaman's highway to Nauta. We were about to visit don Guillermo, a Shipibo Indian who was a well-known ayahuasca healer in this northern Amazonian city. Ayahuasca (*Banisteriopsis caapi*) is a powerful LSD-like woody vine, a plant psychedelic that grows wild in the tropical rain forests of South America and has thousands of years of use in this region of the world. The forest that enclosed don Guillermo's large acreage was full of thin trees and not able to sustain any animal life such as monkeys or other forest creatures.

Here I was, back in the Amazon, back in Iquitos, after an absence of twenty-eight years. When I first came to this thriving city in the late 1960s, I had lived in the squatter settlement of Belen, on a floating houseboat at the edge of the Amazon River. A Peruvian psychiatrist, Dr. Pedro Garcia (a pseudonym), and I were funded to spend the year 1968–69 living in the slum, talking to people about their health and illnesses and learning all we could about the plant psychedelic ayahuasca, traditional medicine, and witchcraft.

There was a tremendous interest in psychedelics—the 1960s were almost over, but scientific interest in these plants and their history of use was very keen in academic circles.

In this book, I will look at my almost forty-five years of scientific studies of plant psychedelics. This was a long journey that brought me

1

An ayahuasca healer's home in Belen.

Street scene in Belen, with salted fish drying in the sun.

(and a colleague, Roger Rumrrill) once again, in 2007, to the doors of an ayahuasca healer to chronicle ayahuasca's use by some twenty-seven other indigenous shamans and urban healers. I was trying to understand the uses and abuses of these powerful, mind-altering plants. It was interesting to see how I literally fell into this research.

Back in New York, where I grew up in a Russian Jewish household with a disdain for religion and spirituality—where not even a bottle of whiskey could be found, with parents who smoked heavily for many years—the names of plant psychedelics were hardly household words. Something of a hardworking prodigy, I graduated from high school in Queens, New York, at fifteen and started college at that young age. My major was psychology, and my early training was heavily loaded with psychoanalytic theories—in fact, in order to graduate from Queens College at that time, one had to pass a test specifically dealing with these theories. Later, when I was a young anthropologist conducting fieldwork in Peru, I came to realize how my background influenced my first experience with ayahuasca in 1968, helping me to see that one's culture determines the content of one's psychedelic experience, and given that, why my particular response to ayahuasca was so different from that of my informants in the slum of Belen.

After a brief marriage that ended when I was twenty-four years old, I decided to return to school for further professional training. I wasn't quite clear about what I wanted to do—perhaps I'd become a social worker and help the downtrodden. I was very good at languages and took three years of French and two years of Spanish in high school, and then seven more semesters of French in college. Being adept at languages would stand me in good stead later on when I decided to go to the Amazon. I enrolled in New York University, where the social-work curriculum was part of the sociology department, which in those days also had an anthropology track. It only took one course on Africa—of great interest to me at the time, given the newly forming nations that had freed themselves from colonial hegemony—to spark my interest in anthropology. I wrote my master's thesis on West African women. Had

I myself been African American, my thesis adviser, Dr. Elliot Skinner, told me, he could have found funds for me to conduct research abroad!

With an M.A. in anthropology in hand, I obtained a teaching position at the University of Massachusetts, with the assumption I would eventually obtain a Ph.D. It was then, while visiting friends in Montreal, that I was introduced to the Peruvian psychiatrist Dr. Garcia who was studying forensics at McGill University. He had grown up in Iquitos, Peru, and on his honeymoon had taken his wife to observe an ayahuasca session in the forest outside of the city. At the time we met he had one more year left to finish his postgraduate work. He was told by his teachers he needed to work with an anthropologist, and I was in need of a dissertation topic. A collaboration was a perfect solution. We decided to work together, which led to the year of research in Iquitos in 1968–69, which was funded by the now-defunct Foundations Fund for Research in Psychiatry.

This was not my first involvement with Peru. During the summer of 1967, before Dr. Garcia and I received our grant, I had lived in a small city called Chiclayo, in northern Peru, which was about an hour and a half south of the village of Salas. The newly founded Institute of Social Psychiatry, in Lima, had provided me with a grant to conduct a brief ethnography of the small rural community of Salas. Dr. Carlos Alberto Seguin, the psychiatrist who was the institute's director, was very interested in the wealth of hallucinogenic plants that abounded in Peru. It was rumored that 100 mestizo men and women in Salas had administered the psychedelic cactus San Pedro (*Trichocereus pachanoi*) to eager visitors and suffering patients.

In Salas, I attended several psychedelic sessions in which San Pedro was boiled into a drink and given to men and women patients. Many of them had journeyed from far away to be treated by the various shamanic healers in Salas. Still enthralled by psychoanalytic theory, I refused to participate, certain that all my deep-seated neuroses that I had learned about in college (after I had to memorize all the defense mechanisms of the ego) would rear their ugly heads and my id would overwhelm me. Moreover, after a conversation I had had with the noted researcher Dr. Michael Harner, who didn't read or write for a year after the Jivaro Indians invited him to drink ayahuasca with a datura-nightshade admixture, I was not about to take any chances.

Unlike many enthusiasts whom we find in the burgeoning field of psychedelics, I always thought that my "fall" into research met the criteria I had learned about in graduate school, that of the German sociologist, Max Weber. He had written about "value-free social science." I had no ax to grind, no particular point of view. Before I met Dr. Garcia, the Peruvian psychiatrist, I had made plans to study Guatemalan Indians who married outside of their community. This would have been a perfectly fine kinship topic for a newly minted anthropologist. Anyhow, I really did like embroidery. That was not about to happen, however, as civil war broke out in Guatemala and anthropologists were being alerted that this was not a good place to do ethnography.

From my initial study in Salas, a number of published articles resulted. After the year in Iquitos came a flow of experiences in which I simply watched other people use hallucinogenic plants for healing, spiritual purposes, divination, and political acumen. At one point the subtitle for this book was *The Boa and Me,* because when asked about my main findings after all these years of studying plant hallucinogens and watching others have psychedelic experiences, I am fascinated by the role of culture in the experience itself. If a person grows up in a setting where plants are believed to be animated by powerful spiritual forces, and, in the case of ayahuasca, if that spirit is a boa constrictor or an anaconda, then the person having a psychedelic experience will most likely experience on the most personal level a vision of that fabulous snake. In the case of other outsiders like myself who take ayahuasca, our visionary experiences will be idiosyncratic—personal, private, and free-floating—and will depend on our background and personal history. As an anthropologist, I am fascinated but not surprised that culture is number one in this equation: that it conditions the nature of one of life's most powerful experiences.

The chapters that follow chronicle the fieldwork I have done in Peru and Brazil. I will talk about my travels and the dissemination of my research findings. At the end of this chronology, I will summarize the results of some of my publications on psychedelic use around the world, which deal with theory, healing, religion, and creativity. A photo archive illustrates the early years of my research, and a glossary will help the reader get a handle on the many Spanish words they will encounter in such a study. The future of psychedelics is always a topic of interest, and I look forward to speculating about the direction of my research in the years to come.

PART ONE

AN OVERVIEW OF MY ANTHROPOLOGICAL LIFE

1

Salas

The Capital of Witchcraft

IN THE SUMMER OF 1967, I began my study of psychedelics in Salas, under psychiatrist Carlos Alberto Seguin, director of the Institute of Social Psychiatry at the University of San Marcos, in Lima. Dr. Pedro Garcia's brother was an engineer who worked in the nearby city of Chiclayo, where I would live during my research. He agreed to accompany me on several visits to Salas.

Getting started in the community was serendipitous. Dr. Seguin's secretary, who hailed from northern Peru, had been very helpful to me when I first arrived. She had a friend who had lived in Salas and who was now in Lima. This woman was kind enough to write me a letter of introduction to her aunt, who still resided in the northern village of Salas. When I arrived in Chiclayo, the nearest city to Salas village, I purchased a small gift for the aunt and called on her. Shortly thereafter, her godson arrived for a visit. He was a notable village elder and businessman in Salas named don Antonio, and he accompanied me there to meet his family.

That summer I spent a lot of time with don Antonio, interviewing ten San Pedro healers. He was quick with introductions and assurances to one and all that I was a good person, a student, wanting to learn about the healing techniques and the power of San Pedro. The first afternoon en route to Salas by car from Chiclayo, don Antonio stopped at a small village where there was a Catholic ceremony honoring the patron saint of the community. On his knees, he traversed the interior of the church's nave to the altar to show his devotion to the saint. He returned to the car, and we went on to Salas.

That night, don Antonio and various visitors who sought out healing for a variety of witchcraft-related illnesses gathered under a small, open shelter called a tambo, with four poles that held up a thatched roof. There a San Pedro healer administered cups of the cactus brew to his patients. Later on I learned that the potion had a high concentration of mescaline. Laid out on the ground was a plastic cloth on which a variety of ritual items had been placed to protect the patients and the healer. Sticks and medieval swords were stuck in the ground as a kind of barrier to keep evil away. There were bottles of herbs and two pots with stirrup handles, placed side by side on the cloth from the Moche culture of the area, dating back to the time of Christ. The healer would blow into the handle using his lip as a reed and make a sonorous sound that no doubt influenced the patients who were under the effects of the San Pedro.

During that summer, over the course of seven to eight weeks, I decided that the best contribution I could make would be a general ethnography of the community. Dr. Seguin had planned to send other researchers to Salas after I finished my base ethnography, including a psychiatrist who would work closely with healers' patients. My job was to understand the context in which San Pedro healing occurred. Unlike a healer who lived in Trujillo, a few hours south, none of the ten healers I worked with were superstars, seeking fame and fortune. I was the only outsider in the community that summer, and because of don Antonio's patronage, I was easily accepted. I was even asked to sit in a place of honor for the July 28 patriotic observances and parade that took place in the community (similar to our Fourth of July celebration).

Over the summer, I interviewed ten of the alleged one hundred healers who lived in Salas. Only two were women, and all of them pleaded poverty. Some of the healers wore very old clothing and ragged shoes. There was a small chapel in the countryside dedicated to Saint

Cipriano, who was said to be the patron of folk healers. Fresh flowers were always placed in the chapel when I went by. Later on I found out that Saint Cipriano was not a canonized saint; rather, history held that he was a Christian martyr during the Roman period who was said to have been thrown to the lions.

Repairing the bridge connecting areas of the slum.

I was able to show that the people of the town of Salas, the "capital of witchcraft," as a newspaper described it that summer, actually lived off tourism. This tourism consisted of men and women from neighboring farming villages and from as far away as Ecuador, a few hours to the north, who came to the town in search of healing. Anthropologists often find a large market town centered in the rural countryside—in this case, Chiclayo. Particular villages radiate outward and specialize in different activities and products. One town in this region, for example, was noted for well-crafted saddlebags; another for the sale of healing herbs. Salas specialized in healing, and it fit comfortably into the network of communities linked to the Chiclayo marketplace.

All too quickly, the summer came to an end and I returned to Lima. By this time, I was curious to visit Iquitos, however briefly, to get some idea of what lay ahead in the coming year if Dr. Garcia and I were able to obtain the funds for the ayahuasca research. Through a contact in the Institute of Social Psychiatry, a social worker in Iquitos was kind enough to take me around the slum of Belen, in the heart of Iquitos. This enabled me to get a good idea of the magnitude of the work ahead.

2

Belen and the Amazon

BACK FROM PERU, IN THE fall of 1967 I spent the next academic year teaching anthropology at California State University, Los Angeles. It was a busy year. My colleague, Dr. Garcia, was still in Montreal, and so from a distance we prepared a grant proposal to enable us to return to Iquitos for one year to study ayahuasca healers and their clients. Since my teaching contract was year to year, if I accepted the grant I knew that at the end of the year I might be without a job and without funds. But I had my family in New York to fall back on if worst came to worst, so I decided to forge ahead. I had completed all the course requirements for a Ph.D. at New York University, so the possibility of using my Amazon research toward a dissertation was very much on my mind. I had no dissertation adviser, however, and I was pretty much on my own. When I returned to California again in 1969, I enrolled at the University of California, Riverside, for the doctoral program and was permitted to use the data I had gathered in Peru after all.

I remember getting ready for my second trip to Peru. Dr. Garcia's cousin in Iquitos had been asked to help me settle in there, after the couple of months I'd be spending in Lima working with Dr. Seguin's team at San Marcos University. I was somewhat apprehensive about going to Iquitos but summoned the courage to do so. I packed a lot of things to take to Peru—some twenty-three cartons of books, dishes, stationery, bed linen, and towels—as if I were off to a wilderness instead of the third- or fourth-largest city in Peru, with a population of about

125,000. These twenty-three cartons would haunt me. On the flight to Peru in June the plane became disabled and was forced to land in Panama. As I deplaned and made my way to the terminal for the trip to Panama City, where we were going to spend the night until a new plane could be dispatched, I saw a pulley from my flight disgorging all twenty-three of my cartons, one by one. Fortunately they all arrived safely, and I ended up leaving some of the boxes behind in Lima with Dr. Garcia's family before making my way to my destination, Iquitos, at the end of July.

The first week or so in Iquitos was very difficult. El Flaco (The Skinny One), Dr. Garcia's cousin, found me a small house to rent about three-quarters of a mile from the slum of Belen, in the heart of Iquitos. It was near the central plaza and the Tourist Hotel, overlooking the Amazon River. El Flaco was a merchant with a small shop on the main street, called Jiron Lima, and he kept any mail that came my way from back home. He actually sold me a motorcycle and a small refrigerator. His father, the mayor of Iquitos, gave me his business card with a note written on the back for the Iquitos Department of Motor Vehicles. It said simply: "Give the gringa a driver's license"—which they grudgingly did. In fact, Dr. Garcia, who drove the Dodge we had budgeted for in the grant, was stopped once by the police, who told him that the car belonged to the gringa!

The motorcycle didn't work out very well, since the carburetor flooded easily, and I got caught in a couple of nasty rainstorms and was repeatedly drenched. I returned the motorcycle and got my money back. Most of the year I was dependent on the small and low-slung buses that went back and forth to the market and to Belen. I felt all alone and tried to decorate my little house in a pleasant manner, despite the fact that the furniture came from a local prison. Some of my colleague's relatives took pity on me and gave me a toucan as a pet. He was a nasty little bird and bit my hand every time I tried to feed him papaya. By that time I was beginning my visits to Belen, with my broad-brimmed sunbonnet to protect me from the penetrating rays of the sun. My Spanish was *mas o menos* by that time, and I could converse easily with people.

In Belen, I chatted with some *ribereños,* river-edge farmers in the city slum, and complained about the toucan. Told to bring the bird to Belen the next day, I went home and in the morning I wrapped the squawking bird in newspaper and took him down to the river's edge. The farmer told me that he would twirl the bird around a large barrel filled with smoking wood and the smoke would help tame it. I was instructed to return the next day to get my about-to-be-domesticated bird back. When I did return, I didn't see the bird anywhere. When I asked where it was, the farmer said: "Que rica la sopa!"—How good the bird soup was!—as he rubbed his belly in delight. That was the end of my bird and my foray into acquiring any pets in an area of the world so poor that the concept of pet as food was the only gloss recognized.

Thus it really surprised me one day as I walked around the slum, stopping to chat with anyone who would hang out with me, to see another bird, rather ugly with long, skinny legs, called a tanrrillo. Later I learned that the bird was an important player in love-magic rituals. Rather than keeping this animal as a pet, this family was holding on to an economic resource that in the future they would sell to a man or woman who would then kill the bird and use the hollow leg bone to secretly gaze at the beloved, recite some spells, and make that person fall madly in love with him or her. If the beloved caught on to the spell, it would ricochet and worsen the bewitcher's obsessions. More on love magic later.

The *barriada* (slum settlement) was quite large, populated by more than 11,000 people. It was divided into three main areas, one of which was called Venecia, named after Venice, in Italy.

The three areas were joined by rickety bridges made of planks. Inevitably as I walked along the different areas I would slip off the bridge planks into the dirty water. I had my trusty small camera wrapped in a thick

A glimpse of Belen where the smell of open sewage was severe.

An area of Belen on the Amazon River.

All along the barriada were poorly constructed houses made of balsa logs with thatched palm fronds for roofing and tree bark peeled off to create walls that were porous.

A balsa raft bringing palm fronds to the slum to sell.

plastic bag to protect it, and the level of the river was quite low at this inlet point.

In the rainy season many of the houses floated in the water, while a second group of houses was built on stilts at a second-story level to keep from flooding in the rainy season. There was some economic activity in the barriada, and I had my favorite haunts where I would stop to have a soda and to chat with the tradesmen and their families.

I decided that I wouldn't mention the word *ayahuasca* first and would wait to see if the plant was on the minds of any of my informants. About three days after I started my meanderings around Belen, one of the farmers asked me if we had ayahuasca in my country. After that, I found that almost everyone I spoke to either had taken ayahuasca at least once in their lives for health purposes or, if they hadn't had an aya-huasca experience, certainly knew about the plant and had heard many tales of other peoples' experiences with it. Mostly the reason for taking "the purge," as it was commonly called, was to diagnose the cause of

Beleños at the river bargaining for produce to resell in the market.

what they believed was a witchcraft hex leveled against them by a rival, an enemy, a family member, or a disgruntled lover.

Some of my informants talked about "allies" that lived in the river, which they could access under the influence of ayahuasca. These *aliados* reminded me of the work I had read shortly before leaving Los Angeles: one of my colleagues had given me the Castaneda book *The Teachings of Don Juan*. When later on in the States there was controversy about the veracity of Castaneda's accounts, I knew that at least, in this regard, Carlos and my informants saw eye to eye.

My day took on a certain rhythm. I would wander down to Belen in midmorning, go from house to house chatting with people, trying to steer the conversation toward ayahuasca but at the same time taking notes on the conversations, noting the economic, family, and value systems of those with whom I interacted.

Dr. Garcia and I had our car available in Iquitos, and we were able to drive the Beleños to ayahuasca sessions. Generally they were held outside the slum at the outskirts of the city where it was quiet and

Plantains for sale to Beleños working in the city market.

A family at a relative's wake.

wooded. We were also available to take them to the many funerals that occurred in Belen. By this time, I was almost thirty years old and had only been to one funeral in my life. Now, in Belen, I could go to a wake (*velorio*) almost every second week if I wanted to. These were very sad occasions.

Once an informant asked me to be the godmother of the umbilical cord of the baby she was due to deliver shortly. I agreed, not knowing what exactly I was supposed to do. When I found out I would be sent for to cut the cord during the delivery, probably in the wee hours of the morning, I decided to leave town for a few days as her due date approached. Such a level of confidence I could live without!

In the beginning of the first two-and-a-half months of fieldwork, the only data I seemed to be getting was laden with sexual innuendo— all about bananas and their ripeness or flaccidity. I wondered what that was all about. But then, a type of conversation with other women would ensue. It started out with questions about my age. I lied a little bit to make myself younger. Certainly the Iquitos sun caused these women to age prematurely as their chores kept them outdoors with little if any protection for their skin. Their response to my stated age was that I looked good because I had no man who kept me under his dominion. And at that moment, a slew of love-magic recipes would spill forth so that I could find a man, come under his dominion, and age quickly like the rest of them.

Not all of this was overtly stated, but a flood of techniques, plants, and activities emerged to help me get and keep a man. When the count reached twenty-five recipes, I felt overwhelmed and took a week off to return to Lima and sit with my little Olivetti typewriter to organize this information, which I then sent off to be published in the *American Journal of Folklore*. It was clear to the Beleños that there was only one kind of love that counted and endured, and that was piggy love (*amor cochinado*) derived from witchcraft. There was even a leaf that a woman was supposed to use to wash her partner's clothing so that he would never leave her side.

During my fieldwork I had to go to San Marcos University in Lima once a month to ensure that the grant money would be paid out in a timely manner. I became friendly with the treasurer's secretary at the university. While I inevitably had to wait in her office for my check to be issued, I would chat with her about all this love-magic lore I was accumulating. She told me the sad story of her daughter who was in love with a fellow who didn't pay her any attention. On the next trip to Lima, I brought the woman an herb called shimi pampana, which her daughter was instructed to chew and put into a bottle of inexpensive Tabu perfume, available in Peru. Every time she was around this fellow, she was to rub it on her body. On the next trip to Lima a month later, I found out that the girl was now engaged to this man and the mother was forever in my debt. This response to suggestion, an important part of shamanic healing, would occur again and again in my research.

I met Yando, my husband of forty years now, early on during my fieldwork. El Flaco had a painting of Yando's in his store and showed it to me. I purchased it, and the family joke is that I'm still paying for it some forty years later! Another joke is that I washed all Yando's clothing with the condorillo leaf so that he would never leave my side! When I met Yando, I told him that I needed an artist to render some drawings of the people with whom I was working, and so we spent time together in Belen and in Iquitos proper.

Yando is the son of Peruvian Amazon healer don Hilde. He grew up witnessing healing practices and also participated in these practices with his father, but he chose art, not healing, as his own profession. He experimented with various plants and their effects, particularly in the context of their effects on art. In his early work he painted while under their influence. All this was for the purpose of exploring the boundaries of art, its expressive and formal possibilities. In the late 1960s and 1970s Yando refused to be part of the art that was then designated "psychedelic art." He has graciously allowed me to include some of his most expressive artwork in this book.

Eventually, when Yando and I decided to move in together, all the love-magic recipes immediately stopped, especially among the family I had become very close to. I ended up renting their balsa-log house in Belen as a second residence to enable me to be closer to my research activities.

One of the daughters, Carla, had been a real source of love-magic recipes. She would take me to fortune-tellers and other specialists in affairs of the heart, telling me to lie about who I was and not talk, she would do all the talking. I was to be on the lookout for some spell to find and capture the soul of a lover. In fact, as I began to interview ayahuasca healers in Belen and visit their consulting areas, I realized that many of the women who came to visit them were eager for the healer to use ayahuasca to retrieve the souls of their partners and return their errant spouses to them. In this culture of poverty, where people didn't know where their next meal was coming from, unstable love relationships were paramount in the lives of women. Specialists who had answers and assumed power to rectify such problems were in high demand.

On occasion, middle-class visitors would come to Belen and act as

The author with two children who had been treated for tuberculosis.

though the inhabitants were invisible. There was a very strong element of racial and class discrimination in this that I found very unsettling as I realized how important skin color, hair, and eye color could be to people quick to pigeonhole others by how they looked.

THE NAIPES

At this time I began to use *naipes,* which are fortune-telling cards that I had learned about in Salas. One night a healer there told his wife to bring the cards down to the tambo where his patients were waiting for the San Pedro ceremony to start. I tried to find out about the cards and how they were used, but the healer brushed me off. I found out that many ayahuasca healers and probably the San Pedro maestro in Salas used the cards as a diagnostic technique in their work, since there were about seventeen misfortune cards that could stimulate a dialog between the person getting a reading and the interpreter, thus giving the healer insight into his client's problems. On a trip to Lima, while meeting with the institute's secretary, I discovered that even though she was solidly middle class, she was quite an aficionada of the cards. I told her of my interest in them, and so she showed me how to read them. I purchased several little books on the naipes in the Chiclayo city marketplace. One supposedly written by Mme Le Normand, reputed to be the adviser to Napoleon, further helped me learn to read each card specifically.

When in Belen one day I took out the naipes, quite small and compact, and began to read the fortune of one of my informants. At the time, it didn't occur to me to ask for any remuneration. After all, these people were so poor, why would I want to burden them any further? However, in November 1968 I left Peru for a meeting of the American Anthropology Association in Seattle, Washington, and stopped first in New York to visit my family. There I visited Ari Kiev, a well-known psychiatrist interested in psychopharmacology. I read his fortune using the naipes (no one has ever accused me of being shy!), and he advised me to request money for my readings, even if it were a small amount, because that was the norm for others who read the cards. In Seattle, anthropologist Michael Harner advised me similarly.

When I returned to Iquitos, I became a full-fledged *curiosa,* a specialist who could divine the future. The power of suggestion was very clear in the readings I did with the naipes; I expect that an ayahuasca healer who used the cards to gain insight into the stressors in a client's world must appear omnipotent. Skill is required to take the discrete items associated with each card and weave them into a story, so that three or four cards read together present a short narrative. Several different readings could be made from many of the cards. In most cases I had to choose the most pertinent reading for the person sitting in front of me. I found myself becoming more flamboyant, dramatizing my readings by hesitating at particular points and exclaiming at still others. I cautioned clients against possible evil in store for them, and

The author telling a fortune with the naipes cards.

I was joyous when good news seemed forthcoming. After I told four or five fortunes in a row, I found myself emotionally drained.

As the demand for my services grew, I opened a consultation

"office" in my balsa-log house, thus launching my official career as a fortune-teller. Suddenly my practice increased tenfold, and people practically lined up to have their fortunes read. At the end of a day of clients' fortunes, I could commiserate with others in the barriada about being so tired after such a hard day's work. Two women with whom I had become friends served as my agents and sent me clients. They kept insisting that I raise my prices, since I only charged the equivalent of a kilogram of rice, a fraction of that collected by my nearest competitor who lived in another area of Iquitos.

Soon, my walk from the Belen market at the city's riverbanks down to the community took a very long time, as people would call me the "gringa who knew things" and pull me into their homes to tell their fortune. People would wake me up early in the morning as they sought advice before making a business decision or going on any trip. During this period, I was depressed—alone, sad, and anxious. Dr. Garcia's friends laughed at me and made jokes at my expense. Later, when I took ayahuasca, all that changed, and I felt able to deal with this unpleasant solitude in which I found myself.

Fortune-telling has always been a marginal topic for anthropologists unless they go into great abstraction about people's needs to understand their anxiety associated with not knowing what the future will bring. All societies have some means of forecasting, whether it's econometrics, to tell when the market is about to nosedive, or fortune-telling cards, to tell you if your lover will ever take you back. After I returned to the States, with the help of some of my colleagues at California State University, Fullerton, I was able to apply a complex mathematical probability equation to the reading of the naipes.

I discovered that the likelihood of at least one misfortune card appearing in a given reading was 99.76 chances in a hundred. Wow! That two misfortune cards would occur went down to 97.4 chances in a hundred, and the likelihood that at least three misfortune cards would appear in a given reading was 87.7 chances in a hundred. The numbers fell off precipitously after that. Each card read is modified by

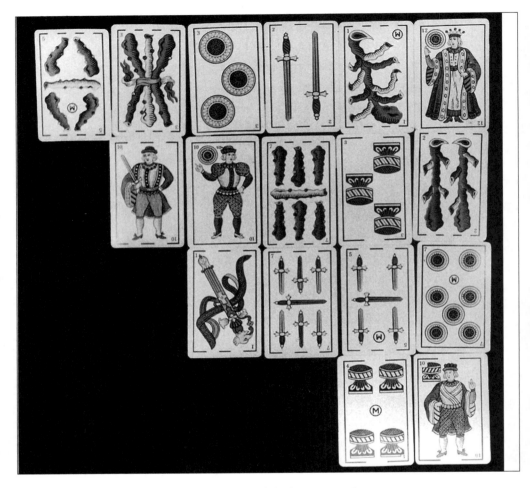

Seventeen naipes cards laid out in a reading.

the preceding and sequential cards. Any interpreter could quite easily construct a story line that focuses on interpersonal conflict, material loss, or illness. Thus the deck is effectively stacked not in the direction of good fortune, but as fortune's malice—to highlight the stress and conflict in the client's world. Thus a healer, reading the fortune of a client who suffers from some psychosomatic disorder, could have a clear expectation of tapping in to the source of the problems.

When I later published on the fortune-telling data I had assembled, I called the article "Fortune's Malice" to describe a little-known trait of fortune-telling cards—namely, that malevolence and bad luck is ever present in a card reading. When examined through the lens of probability statistics, one sees that the average deck of Peruvian naipes has up to seventeen of the forty cards that are interpreted as bringing misfortune, such as false pregnancies, business losses, and even death. Since folk healers who use ayahuasca treat a large number of psychosomatic disorders in their clients, these misfortune cards can be an effective means of uncovering culturally induced stresses that contribute to the psychosomatic disorders that clients face. This is especially true when people in Peru "dialog" with the cards, that is, commenting on all sorts of private information about who is angry at me and who wants me to suffer. This could be a mother-in-law, for example, or an ex-lover. After the initial reading, three questions may be asked by the client, and the curiosa alternately turns cards face up. If the ace of diamonds appears, the answer to a question is affirmative.

I call the naipes an "ethno-projective device," comparable to other Western psychotherapeutic techniques such as the Thematic Apperception Test (TAT) and the Rorschach. The naipes, however, transcend the problem of using a test developed in the West to learn about personality variables of people from traditional cultures. Culturally neutral, the naipes contain symbols and meanings that are relevant to both the healer and his patients, both of whom share a Third World culture that is laden with poverty, illness, suffering, and despair. In Peru the naipes have been used at least since colonial times by healers and their patients, who live in a world of magical causality of disease, where witchcraft and hexing are widespread beliefs. This tool permits entry into the private world of the person. At the very least, the cards are a useful analytical device for the anthropologist who is attempting to uncover prevalent themes in the society she is studying, as well as affording her insight into how folk psychotherapy works.

At the meeting of the American Anthropological Association in Seattle in November 1968, I discovered that I would be on a panel with

Michael Harner, Carlos Castaneda, and others associated with the field of hallucinogenic/shamanic research and here I was, never, ever having taken ayahuasca myself. By the same token, Dr. Garcia had been given 100-microgram capsules of LSD by the pharmaceutical company Sandoz before he went to Canada. He was able to locate two capsules, one for my husband, Yando, and one for myself, before my trip to Seattle. Foolishly, we took the LSD on a Thursday and visited a healer in Belen on the following Tuesday for an evening dose of ayahuasca. I was curious to see if Western "magic" was more powerful than Peru's.

The purge, as it is so well named, is very hard on the body. I was told to eat lightly and avoid certain foods before ingesting ayahuasca. Basically, I had the dry heaves during the entire session, along with severe diarrhea. I touched the arm of Yando, who was with me at the beginning of the session, and saw a cornucopia of visions, while that night Yando did not have any visions of his own. Apparently it's a no-no to touch another person or else one gets a double dose. Since Yando was the son of a healer, he had already had many ayahuasca experiences, but due to my faux pas, not on the night we took it together!

The balsa on which we were seated was tied to a small cliff overlooking the water, and I remember wanting to jump in the river because of the effects of the purge. The visions were very personal, and I never saw the mother spirit of the plant—the boa—because I hadn't ever really seen a boa up close in my lifetime. Rather, I saw trick-or-treat green and orange flags waving at me, a childhood memory of that joyful Halloween holiday and the candy that goes with it. However, I did see a woman sneering at me, which my informants in Belen later told me was an envious woman who probably wanted to bewitch me. As the healer made percussive sounds in the air with his *schacapa,* a bunch of wild grasses held together by a vine, he kept telling me that the music would evoke more calming visions in the moments to come. This cued me to the important role of the whistling incantations, *icaros,* and the role of drumming to influence a person's visions. Psychologists call this synesthesia, a scrambling of sensory modalities. I remember at the end of the session waiting for a taxi to take us back to our house in Iquitos, with pain in my eyeballs from the city lamp near the bench on which we rested.

My LSD experience the previous week, by contrast, had been very muted and laden with psychoanalytic thoughts and feelings from my past. When I looked in the mirror in my house in the city where Yando and I took the LSD, I saw my mother staring back at me in my reflection. Since our relationship had been somewhat conflicted, I saw myself becoming her in the future. That was disconcerting. However, in the years to come, I was able to deal with her in a more forgiving manner than before I went to Peru.

In Seattle our symposium on hallucinogens went well, and I was pleased to have a break from the intensity of the research I had been involved in. It was at that meeting that I was interviewed for a teaching position at California State University, Fullerton; I was subsequently offered the position, which would begin once my year's research in Iquitos was finished.

Since the Amazon was so hot and sticky, and my short hair always looked frizzy, I purchased a wig, which was all the vogue that year. I took it to Seattle with me. I also bought a very elegant red plaid dress with a black bodice and a matching plaid shawl, which I wore for my interview with the Cal State Fullerton recruiter. Later on I was told by a gossipy colleague that the department had been pressured to hire some women instructors. When my application was up for review, someone noted that I had published two scholarly papers on the Salas and Belen data. I learned that there was some question as to whether I was serious in my research. The man who interviewed me said: "Oh no, she looks like a model, and I don't think we have to worry about serious scholarship!"

When I returned to Iquitos after the anthropology meetings in November 1968, Dr. Garcia and I drifted apart in our interests and activities. I realized that I would probably have to publish by myself without any backup from him. The following spring, since the rainy season made continued field research impossible, I returned to Lima to conduct library research on ayahuasca and to write up my findings. The teaching position at Cal State Fullerton was waiting, and so Yando and I left Peru in June 1969 for the twenty-four-hour flight to California, via Venezuela and Miami. I remember that there were squawking monkeys on board as we made our way to Miami and then to Los Angeles. The next decade would be one that would make sense of all that I had experienced and learned in Belen.

3

The 1970s

THE YOUNG WOMAN WHO CAME back to California from the Amazon was not the same one who had interviewed for the job in Seattle. Instead of a svelte anthropologist thin from the ravages of hookworm, with runway hair owing to a sleek wig, the woman who appeared in California to start her job had short, frizzy hair, a regular girth (now that she no longer had hookworm), and a soon-to-be husband at her side. The hookworm and I had coexisted for about half a year in Iquitos and Lima. I probably got the parasite when I slipped and fell down in the wet mud one afternoon in Belen. Hookworm can enter through the skin, I later learned. Yando and I were on our way to a new restaurant in Iquitos, which had a paper mural on the wall for all the establishment's well-wishers to write their little poem or story on. I inked in the following in Spanish: "I dedicate this poem to the poor people of Belen, slipping through the streets of their lives."

Shortly after that incident, I went to Lima to seek treatment for the lethargic effects of the parasite. The only help I received was from a "specialist" in tropical medicine who prescribed some iron pills. Toward the end of my stay in Lima during the spring of 1969, I was interviewing a public-health physician who had conducted research in Iquitos. We were chatting away in Spanish when he told me that even middle-class people in the Amazon suffered from *anquilostoma* (hookworm). I became excited and said in Spanish, "Doctor, I, too, have anquilostoma." He changed to English and said, "Miss Dobkin: you have hookworm!" Then he gave me a prescription for some poison I had to take twice, once that same week in Peru and then a month later when we returned to the United States, to kill off the worms. I now understood why the children in Belen had such a low energy level. This also made it clear why ayahuasca would be so popular a purge—it was nature's way of getting rid of the worms, which apparently didn't like the taste of ayahuasca very much and left their host posthaste. I later found out that a California biochemist, Eloy Rodriguez, had discussed this link in a scientific paper he published in the 1970s. All I could think of was that now "they" had to give me my Ph.D., since I had sacrificed my liver to science . . .

Yando and I settled into a small house in Fullerton. We got married, and I began teaching cultural anthropology at Cal State Fullerton. The following summer of 1970, Michael Harner recommended me for a position as visiting scientist at the Smithsonian Institution, which was mounting an exhibit called "Toward Understanding Man's Use of Drugs." Some two million people were expected to attend. Yando and I drove across the county, the first of three such trips over the years, in our new Chevy, and we spent that summer in Washington, D.C. It was a very exciting time for me. I had an impressive title and access to the museum's collections. Yando's training in fine arts and my growing knowledge of the ethnographic role of plant psychedelics worked very well together, and I quickly had a list of cultures where such plants had historically been integrated into religious and healing activities. I met one of the officials of the National Commission on Marijuana and Drug Abuse and was given a contract for the following year, 1971, to prepare a report on the non-Western use of psychedelics. This later became my second book, first titled *The Wilderness of Mind* and subsequently retitled *Hallucinogens: Cross-cultural Perspectives.*

Early in my career I realized that I would have to obtain a doctorate or I would not have much of a future in academia. I enrolled at the University of California, Riverside, and was able to complete my Ph.D. by 1972, using the ayahuasca materials I had gathered in Peru for my dissertation. Every seminar I took at the University of California,

Riverside, transformed into one chapter of the dissertation, and I was able to finish the coursework in two years and wait out my committee members' readings and rewrites during a third year. That year of 1972 was a banner year for me: I received my Ph.D., gave birth to a baby girl, Gabriela, and received tenure at Cal State Fullerton, where I would remain, with some forays out and back, for the next thirty years.

In November 1971, when I was five months pregnant with my daughter, I went to Mexico to attend the Fifth World Congress of Psychiatry, where I reported on my research with ayahuasca. I was busy writing up my data, and although I didn't return with multiple boxes of field notes, the flow of ideas was constant. My book on ayahuasca, Visionary Vine, had been published a few months before I submitted my Ph.D. dissertation. After taking ayahuasca in Peru, I felt like a tap had opened with regard to my writing, and I became very productive.

As a doctoral candidate at UC Riverside, I had to prepare three research papers in anthropology rather than the traditional task of sitting for comprehensive exams. This seemed to be a much more positive approach to learning than simply memorizing kinship variations and other esoteric anthropological theories. One of my papers for the subfield of archaeology dealt with the ancient Maya. My hypothesis was that the Maya used psychedelic plants as part of their religious rituals.

This was the beginning of my research into an area of historical importance—namely, trying to demonstrate the impact of plant psychedelics on human prehistory. I did this by examining ancient art, architecture, and cultural artifacts such as ceramics and textiles. From 1969 to 1972, I conducted library research on the Maya's use of three hallucinogens: mushrooms, the water lily, and the skin of the common *Bufo alvarius* toad. The water lily's psychedelic property, little known, was suggested to me by the botanist at the L.A. County Museum of Natural History, Dr. William Emboden. My supervisor at UC Riverside asked me to confer with some of his colleagues at the University of California, Berkeley, which I did. They were very polite but not at all convinced.

Sometime later, I heard that American hippies were wandering around the Yucatán chewing the rhizomes of the water lily.

I went to a dinner party in Mexico City with friends at the American Anthropological Association's meeting in 1973 and met Mexican biochemist José Luis Diaz. Independently of my own work on the water lily, he had analyzed the rhizomes of the water lily *Nymphaea ampla,* which is a frequent motif in Mayan art, even more so than the symbol for the rain god. Diaz was able to identify the presence of an opiate-like chemical called aporphine. After causing heavy purging in a person, it creates a languid, visionary state. We collaborated the following year at a meeting of the Latin American Psychiatry Association, where our research findings were presented. I was able to write a rejoinder to the scholarly disdain expressed in the journal *Current Anthropology,* where I first published my hypothesis in 1974. At that time, several notable Mayanists were vituperative in arguing that their beloved Maya would never have used psychoactive substances.

The journal *New Scholar* published my rejoinder, and the hard scientific evidence that we had on the lily brought the argument to an end. Nonetheless, Mayanists continued to ignore this line of reasoning for many years. This early attempt of mine to extrapolate back in time in order to understand the important role that plant psychedelics had in human history was exciting but very demanding of me, especially since it required archaeological and botanical expertise to be certain that there was sufficient evidence.

This approach, however, was speeded along by the earlier work I had done for the Second National Commission on Marijuana and Drug Abuse. For that report, I had delineated a series of themes that related to psychedelic use cross-culturally. By using these themes and documenting the availability of plant psychedelics to ancient peoples, one could make a reasonable conclusion of psychedelic use by ancient cultures through an examination of their art.

In 1972 I met with Dr. Daniel Feldman, a psychiatrist at the University of California, Irvine, a half-hour drive from Fullerton. We collaborated on an alcohol research project among Latino residents of Orange County, California, where Dr. Feldman ran the county alcoholism unit, which was then independent of the county mental health facilities. My skills in Spanish and my comfort in working with Latino immigrants blended well with his considerable expertise, and we wrote a grant that was funded by the National Institute of Alcoholism and Alcohol Abuse (NIAAA). I spent the next year, 1973–74, working closely with mental-health professionals who specialized in alcohol abuse.

I decided to focus on the sociocultural context of alcohol use. I realized that I needed to learn all I could about altered states of consciousness, and not only psychedelic ones, for a complete overview. Dr. Andrew Weil's book on altered states, *The Natural Mind* (1972), was very influential. The ubiquity of such states, I thought, must have some important Darwinian implications for species survival. I obtained a summer fellowship in neurobiology and addictions (to allow me to be a better consumer of the scientific literature) in 1977, and eventually I studied hypnosis at a major regional hospital. This helped round out my understanding of these nonordinary states.

I also received a grant in the mid-1970s from the National Institute of Mental Health to work with biofeedback at the University of California, San Francisco. Dr. David Smith, an authority on the psychopharmacology of drugs and the founder of the Haight-Ashbury Free Clinic, offered me the use of a biofeedback laboratory at the university, and I spent the academic year writing and learning about yet another altered state. I became a member of the advisory board of the *Journal of Psychoactive Drugs* at that time, and over the years I have encouraged young scholars to submit anthropological papers to the journal on indigenous cultures' use of psychedelic plants in healing, witchcraft, botany, and divination.

In San Francisco, a neighbor of mine who was a yoga adept took me to her ashram one day to learn some of the asanas. It was a very sweaty experience and hard for me. When it was her turn to learn some biofeedback techniques, she assured me that the results gave the same level of relaxation and inner calm, but without all the sweating!

In 1978–79 I lived for a year in Lima, Peru, with Yando and Gabriela, who was now six years old, directing a university overseas program. I worked closely with the Septrionic mystical-philosophical order in Lima, which I learned about from Yando's father, Don Hilde, in order to learn self-development techniques and meditation. I found this to be so helpful and engaging that we eventually set up a nonprofit religious organization when we returned to California; we have continued our Tuesday evening meditations and translations of this wisdom tradition right up to the present.

As I read everything that I could find on ayahuasca and the Peruvian Amazon in the UC Berkeley Library during 1975–76, I realized that one of the major explanations for non-Western use of plant psychedelics dealt with their presumed powers of divination. When ayahuasca was first brought under scientific scrutiny in the early part of the twentieth century, the active principle was named telepathine for its suggested power to enable people under the influence to experience telepathy and retrocognition (the latter being a person's ability to see into the past in order to understand something that is happening in the present). Later the researchers found that the alkaloid already had been described as harmine, and so the telepathine label was dropped.

I thought it would be interesting to explore this parapsychology aspect further. After all, most of the men and women I spoke with in Belen went to an ayahuasquero for help because they believed that the cause of their illness was due to witchcraft. The visionary states under ayahuasca revealed to them a panorama of events, a theater of the mind where they would see an evildoer slipping some potion into their beer to cause them to become bewitched and to suffer all kinds of negative consequences. The Beleños often said to me that ayahuasca was better than the movies: it makes you see things . . .

One woman recounted how a rejected boyfriend bewitched her and caused her to become an alcoholic. Under the influence of ayahuasca she was able to identify this as the source of her illness. The ayahuasca shaman she worked with, also under the influence, returned the evil to her ex-boyfriend; only then did he treat the woman's alcoholism with plant medicines.

Given my own long-standing interest in parapsychology, I organized three symposia in the 1970s on parapsychology and culture. These were in the continuing education departments at UC Berkeley, UCLA, and UC Irvine. I invited a number of anthropologists with field experience in cultures with beliefs in witchcraft, magic, and animism to try to build a theory in parapsychology that would include the so-called powers of the psychedelics to enhance such behaviors and beliefs. Unfortunately, we didn't reach any major conclusions. It would take neurobiological imaging to try to understand the centuries of anecdotal reports. What I was able to garner from these meetings was that the doors of perception were truly open for the person taking plant psychedelics like ayahuasca; one became much more sensitive in scanning one's environment, using all the senses in a way that perhaps has fallen into disuse in modern urban life. Here, pollution and the numerous toxins of society are ubiquitous. In recent years, for example, I have become an aficionada of the work of clinical psychologist Paul Ekman, who writes about the enormous amount of information we can access if we simply learn to read people's facial expressions and body language.

In November 1973, I participated in the American Anthropological Association meeting in Mexico City. The paper I gave, titled "Is Science Catching Up with Magic?" was part of a symposium on parapsychology. I was interested in water witching—finding underground water by means of a dowsing rod—including its physical explanations, plant perceptions (interspecies communication, as they now call it), and other parapsychological topics that perhaps had physical explanations. However, I was even more interested in the subtle responses of the human organism to problem solving that may look magical but is actually based on reason.

The best example of magical behavior I can think of occurred not

in the Amazon, where I sat around and watched people take psychedelics, but rather in a lecture hall at Long Beach Memorial Hospital,
where I studied hypnosis. Each week a different lecturer would illustrate the medical and dental aspects of hypnosis. The kind, elderly dentist who came to lecture one Friday asked the audience of some eighty
psychotherapists (I was the only nonlicensed professional there) if someone who suffered a gag effect would volunteer to be the subject of a
hypnotic-induction technique.

One woman responded, and the dentist quickly hypnotized her and
with his little wooden tongue depressor showed us her gag reaction.
Then he placed her in a hypnotic trance again and suggested that she
no longer had to worry, that she would react normally like everyone
else, when the depressor was placed in her mouth. He demonstrated
this much to everyone's amazement. Then he returned her gag response,
which he explained was to show the woman that she was indeed in control of her own body processes. Finally he removed the gag response
for good. I don't know about my peers, but I kept asking the volunteer
about her gag response in the weeks that followed, and she reported
that she no longer suffered from this problem. This illustration of the
power of suggestibility in a healing setting was to pique my interest con-
siderably in the years to come, especially once I began to understand its
link with plant-psychedelic use.

In 1974 I was invited to a government-sponsored cannabis research
conference at the University of Chicago. My paper examined the role of
peoples' beliefs, values, and expectations when they used a powerful psychedelic chemical and how these could enable us to predict the person's
psychedelic reaction. I remember sitting next to a man from Pakistan at
a meal, and in an incredulous tone of voice he told me that the paper I
had just presented that afternoon was too theoretical: it was almost as if
I had the jump on researchers in this field, given the time I had already
spent in Salas and Iquitos.

After spending a year working with several ayahuasca healers, I
decided to evaluate more closely one healer in particular: my father-

in-law, don Hildebrando Rios. In 1977, when I had a sabbatical from teaching for one semester, and then again in 1978–79 when I ran an overseas program in Peru for several universities, my family and I were able to spend time in Pucallpa, Peru, at the home of my father-in-law. don Hilde, as he was affectionately known, was a well-regarded ayahuasca healer in that city. I had first met him in 1969, in a brief visit that Yando and I paid him. I very much wanted to undertake a formal study of his ayahuasca activities, particularly to learn more about his clients and their experiences, and I wanted to also compare the way he treated patients who came to his home office with the methods of the shamans I knew in Iquitos.

Even to this day, the only reports we often have available in the academic literature about ayahuasca healing concern foreigners who visit healers and their responses to the psychedelics like ayahuasca (see chapter 13). Certainly when I was in the field in 1977 little had been written about the mestizo men and women in large cities like Pucallpa who went to ayahuasca healers to be treated for a variety of witchcraft-related illnesses.

Before I left Fullerton for Pucallpa, I put together a twenty-five-item questionnaire for don Hilde's clients, including their background, social class, education, occupation, and symptoms as well as their ayahuasca experiences. Most of his clients had already seen medical doctors in the city prior to seeing the healer. Most sociological studies of patient populations have to confront the question of sampling, that is, Is the number of people who respond to the questions truly representative of the "universe" of people in this milieu? Since I was the daughter-in-law, I acted in the capacity of a nurse. Don Hilde would not see his patient unless the person sat with me first and responded to my questionnaire.

In that way I obtained data on ninety-five men and women who came to see don Hilde during one month's time in 1979. Later on I was able derive correlations between different traits, such as years of education and belief in witchcraft, percentages of referrals to don Hilde by satisfied clients, and so on. I went on to publish a book, *Amazon Healer: The Life and Times of an Urban Shaman,* in 1992 as well as several articles in academic journals. There was one article published on the vidente phenomenon, which is the widespread belief in the highly regarded, presumed psychic powers of a healer. I had heard about this phenomenon in a lecture at the University of Miami given by Dr. Staniford, then of the National Institute of Mental Health. The phenomenon was known as a "biology of hope"—a phrase coined by the late Norman Cousins. (There will be a more detailed discussion of this in chapter 7.)

As a form of suggestibility, I found that this occurred again and again among ayahuasca patients. Almost all the patients who came to see don Hilde had been brought to his clinic by a satisfied customer. I also was able to learn about the plants that don Hilde used to treat a variety of illnesses. His list of plants and the types of illnesses he treated were very impressive. At that time, I estimated that from an ethnographic perspective about 65 percent of the world's population had access to traditional medicine such as the type offered by don Hilde. Clearly many such interventions were without psychedelic plants but probably with some techniques or substances to alter waking consciousness and alleviate anxiety or stress.

Don Hilde was truly a visionary. He would enter into a light trance, occasionally speaking in a strange tone of voice that he later said were the voices of plant spirits speaking through him. He claimed that his inspiration for treatment came during the ayahuasca sessions that he offered several times a month.

I never took ayahuasca again after that experience in Belen in 1968, although every Tuesday night don Hilde would conduct a session that I would attend. I remember being asked to leave one time when I was menstruating: there was a general belief that menstrual blood was polluting, which I thought probably dated back to hunting-and-gathering times when women were not included in the hunt due to their body's reproductively linked odors.

Certainly ayahuasca, like all psychedelics, enhanced all the senses, including smell. Women typically did not become ayahuasca healers themselves until after menopause. In the entire year that I worked with Beleños, I only saw one older woman assist a maestro with the icaros, the shamanic power songs used to communicate with the spirits of the natural world. Women who were involved with clients often played the role of *bruja* (witch) and prepared potions, called *pusangas,* to make a man fall in love with the client, to return back to his spurned lover, or to become impotent if he had sex with anyone besides that woman. Those potions were widely feared, and I was constantly told by my informants not to buy any soft drink prepared by street vendors because they were potential sources of bewitchment.

As part of my duties at the overseas-students program I directed in Lima in 1978–79, I acted as a house mother and registrar. Most of the students were away from home for the first time and were anxious and impetuous. After about the third month, one of the students came to see me to complain about the drug abuse of many students in the program. I almost closed down the program as a result, but we were able to hire a lawyer to provide some protection in case any of the students were arrested or got into trouble. Apparently, the Napoleonic Code in Peru, unlike its counterpart in English jurisprudence, assumes guilt before innocence is proved. My fear was guilt by association— that because of my research interests I felt that I was a real patsy who would be blamed if anything went wrong. In fact, I often wondered if the reason I was chosen for the job was due to someone's supposition that I had a personal commitment to the use of psychedelics. The drug that students were attracted to was cocaine, freely available in the society. Fortunately, nothing of consequence happened to the students that year, and we were able to return home without any incidents. The program shut down for a month's vacation in February, at which time my family and I moved to Pucallpa to live with don Hilde for the month.

During the spring of 1979, I was asked by the American embassy's cultural attaché to help plan the First World Congress of Folk Medicine, which was to be held in November of that year at three sites in Peru: Lima, Iquitos, and Cuzco. I helped to promote the conference abroad and was later given a Fulbright Travel Award to attend. People came from all over the world, and there was real interest in learning about ayahuasca and other Peruvian hallucinogenic plants.

In the late 1970s I traveled to Miami, Seattle, San Francisco, Wisconsin, San Diego, and Fresno and published numerous papers on ayahuasca, on archaeology, and on altered states. I also became concerned about the future of anthropology as a discipline and somewhat envious of those who were healers versus those of us who studied healing. This would change for me in the 1980s, when I returned to graduate school to obtain a second master's degree, this time in clinical psychology. As a practicing psychotherapist in my own culture, I was determined to salvage what I could from the shamanic healing I had studied and apply this knowledge to patients in Southern California.

4

The 1980s

IN 1980 MEDICAL ANTHROPOLOGIST Margaret Clark, my postdoctoral supervisor in the Medical Anthropology Program at the University of California, San Francisco, recommended that I apply for a position as a health-science administrator in a research training unit at the National Institute of Mental Health. I was offered the job and took a leave of absence from my teaching at Cal State Fullerton, sold our house, found a home for our two dogs, and off we went to Rockville, Maryland. I remember my daughter complaining that we had moved five times in seven years! In my new position I had responsibility for some major research programs around the country that were funded by the institute. My background studying plant psychedelics was rarely discussed among my peers, and I settled in as a bureaucrat to learn the job.

I realized early on that I missed teaching, but I tried to make the best of this new activity. I did have time to write and reflect on what really interested me in the ayahuasca materials I still wanted to publish. The task seemed endless. During the eighteen months that I was in the Washington, D.C., area, I was able to complete my manuscript on don Hilde and his plants and patients, which would lead to the publication of my book *Amazon Healer* in 1992.

The position I had in Washington, D.C., was a GS-14, probably equivalent to a dean as far as salary went. I joked with my friends and relatives that the president of the United States was a GS-18, so watch out! Actually, I couldn't wait to return to teaching, which I did when

43

Ronald Reagan became president and there was a staff reduction in the agency. A number of people were to be demoted to a thirty-two-hour week with few benefits, and I was one of the last hired before a freeze on positions was instituted. I still had my teaching position on hold in California, and so we happily returned to Fullerton in the summer of 1981.

I kept feeling like my parents did when they described their experiences of the Great Depression—jobs were hard to find and easy to lose. The tenure system at the university worked really well in my case, because it gave me the academic freedom to research areas that were seen as marginal—namely, psychedelics and culture—although I did forge ahead and receive promotions in a timely manner given my active research record. I had made some good contacts in my government job, and when I was back at Fullerton I even worked for a few years as the director of university research, to encourage faculty to submit grants. But the die was cast, and for the next twenty-five years or so I would continue my research on plant psychedelics, along with my teaching and psychotherapy activities.

Most of the eighties were spent working with therapeutic issues derived from traditional healing. I organized a symposium in Washington, D.C., for the American Association for the Advancement of Science on "anthropology and therapeutic epistemologies," or, in other words, How do we know things about healing? I continued to disseminate my research findings on ayahuasca healing and gave talks in Los Angeles, in Baltimore (at Johns Hopkins University), as well as at various universities. Settled back in at Cal State Fullerton, I was invited by a psychology colleague, Joyce Friedman, to consult at the burn center of the University of California, Irvine, Medical Center. Here a large percentage of the patients were Spanish-speaking immigrants suffering work-related burns. My background in Peru with the urban poor stood me in good stead as I began my therapy career, first as a hypnotherapist working with pain control. Eventually I would complete my second M.A. in clinical psychology. By 1986 I obtained my state psychotherapy counseling credential, and I began to see patients part time both at the hospital and in a small private office I opened in Fullerton.

My psychedelic research continued unabated. In the fall of 1984 I presented a paper at the University of Illinois at Chicago Circle to the Association of American Hispanic Psychiatrists on Amazonian plant pharmacopoeias. In California, I tried to use the insights I had garnered from shamanic healing in my work with the culturally diverse population of Latino laborers. Hypnosis was to be an important and legally available component toward creating an altered state of consciousness that I could use clinically in the service of health.

In the spring of 1987 I presented five lectures at the Bowers Museum, a cultural arts facility in Santa Ana, California. Here I applied the data I had assembled in my class lectures to discussions of the tribal arts. From the mid 1970s on I had developed two courses that incorporated my knowledge of psychedelics in examining various world cultures where such plants had an integral role in religion and healing. One of the classes was called Comparative Aesthetics and Symbolism, and the other was a class on Native American cultures north of Mexico. I also enjoyed teaching world ethnographies, where I would select specific cultures to study that had a history of psychedelic-plant use. At first the students were embarrassed by the scholarly approach to the topic, but they quickly realized that one could fail a test on cannabis's history, for example, if they didn't study the readings and lecture notes just like any other topic in anthropology.

Throughout the 1980s I reported on my research in traditional healing. Some of my talks were local while others took place in Quebec, Phoenix, Miami, and Madison, Wisconsin. In July 1988, I was able to present information in Spanish on don Hilde's healing with ayahuasca at the International Congress of Americanists, held in Amsterdam. I gave a lecture on hallucinogens and art for the psychiatry department of the University of California, Irvine, and argued that traditional cultures didn't focus much on displaying plant psychedelics in their art but rather focused on the religious and spiritual themes that were provoked by such ingestion. My early work on cross-cultural hallucinogens delineated a series of themes linked to plant hallucinogenic use across time and space. I argued that if we knew that plant psychedelics were available for use in a given area, we could reconstruct their use in societies that are now extinct. Themes that characterized numerous societies, to be discussed later in this book, serve as a key to unlocking a complex iconography in the art.

Psychiatrist and psychedelic researcher Dr. Charles Grob and I were invited by the Society for Humanistic Psychology to present an hour's talk each on psychedelics and healing at the American Psychological Association meeting in New Orleans in 1989. There was a growing interest in the medical use of these substances as well as interest by anthropologists. The studies I had conducted on don Hilde, while anecdotal and correlational in nature, nonetheless were the data we had available, since research with psychedelics in the United States and Europe had been prohibited since the 1960s. Dr. Grob and I spoke to a full house in New Orleans.

That same year, I was invited to a conference of the International Transpersonal Association in northern California by Dr. Stanislav Grof, one of the founders of transpersonal psychology and a pioneering researcher in altered states of consciousness. I presented a lecture on psychedelics and art. This audience was much more open to my work than many of the academic ones I had addressed.

The eighties were to be a very productive period in terms of my research, which was mainly focused on traditional healing, shamanism, and how to derive psychotherapy techniques based on our knowledge of Amazonian therapeutics. I continued to examine the psychedelic materials and disseminate my findings in my teachings at Cal State Fullerton and in the occasional lecture that came my way. My interests in pre-Colombian cultures and the impact of plant psychedelics persisted as I published articles on the Moche and Nazca cultures of coastal Peru.

In 1989 anthropologist Michael Winkelman and I coedited a

133-page issue of the *Journal of Psychoactive Drugs* dealing with shamanism and altered states of consciousness. We invited a number of scholars to contribute, and the issue quickly sold out. I included a chapter detailing the plant medicines don Hilde used in his therapy practice in Pucallpa.

5

The 1990s

DURING THE 1990S I WAS in full gear with my psychotherapy activities. For a year and a half I was the transcultural specialist for the psychiatry department at UC Irvine, at their teaching site at Metropolitan State Hospital in Norwalk, California. There I helped organize a lecture series on culture and health for all levels of clinical staff. I continued for seven more years as director of counseling at the UC Irvine Regional Burn Center, offering my services without charge. I provided interpretation for the Monday burn clinic, where more than half the patients were Spanish-speaking immigrants. Occasionally I would be referred to an insured client, whom I would see for pain control and would incorporate hypnotherapy in the treatment. In April 1990, I was invited to lecture on shamanism and psychedelics at the University of New Mexico in Albuquerque. I spent a week that year at the Rim Institute near Payson, Arizona, at a conference on epistemology organized by the artist Gilah Hirsch. This period marked the flowering of interest in my psychedelic research in the broader, New Age community. Men and women on personal quests, not simply interested in research for its own sake, were an eager audience, although I continued to write articles for peer-reviewed journals in my field.

In October 1990, I went to Timberline Lodge, near Portland, Oregon, for a meeting of the Society for the Study of Psychiatry and Culture. There I presented a paper coauthored with Dr. Grob on adolescent drug use and abuse. We examined three traditional tribal societies that used psychedelic substances for their suggestibility properties, to quickly effect bonding among youth who needed to share resources to survive in their culture. The audience was less than impressed and found our focus on traditional cultures' use of psychedelics as agents to inculcate values and beliefs in their young people unpleasant to contemplate.

Around this time, on the recommendation of the psychiatrist Roger Walsh, I was promoted to associate clinical professor of psychiatry at UC Irvine. I gave occasional lectures on Latino mental health to psychiatric residents and fellows, and the occasional hospital grand rounds included my discussions of traditional healing with psychedelics that was part of the lived experience of many Latino laborers we see in Southern California. One grand rounds I presented, both at UC Irvine and Harbor/UCLA Medical Center, looked at lessons from shamanic healing: brief pschotherapy with the Latino immigrant client.

During this decade I also read grants for the Social Sciences and Humanities Research Council of Canada and reviewed manuscripts for journals such as *Social Science and Medicine* and the *Journal of Psychoactive Drugs*. In 1991 I spent a long weekend at Stanford University at the Bridge Conference, a student-sponsored conference, where I spoke about my research with hallucinogens, shamanism, psychedelics, creativity, and the arts. It was a very disappointing conference, not from the point of view of the presenters, who were excellent, but the audience, who left a lot to be desired. Here I encountered the youthful zealots whose motto appeared to be "make more, use more drugs." Nevertheless, Dr. Grob and I subsequently tried to interest an audience at UCLA Extension in discussions of art and altered states of consciousness from a panel of guest speakers, but the turnout was quite small.

In Temecula, California, I attended an Anthropology of Consciousness conference under the aegis of the American Anthropological Association, where several European scholars shared their research findings. German scholars were very keen on learning more about the role of psychedelics in traditional societies and I was able to publish a number of research papers in both English and German in Germany (others translated the works into German for me). In 1991 I received a travel award from the German government's Academic Exchange Program to tour several German cities, including Cologne, Heidelberg, and Düsseldorf. In the Museum of the City of Cologne, I examined Peruvian coastal pottery I believed was connected to San Pedro psychedelic use; I also gave several lectures on my psychedelic research work, one at the Heidelberg Medical School.

By this time several of my papers had been translated and published in Germany, and there was a real interest in psychedelic research in that country. So the following year, 1992, I was invited to Göttingen, Germany, to the European Congress for Consciousness Studies. En route to Germany, I gave a talk in Ghent, Belgium, on my psychedelic research, which was funded by the Belgium National Science Foundation.

The Göttingen symposium was attended by more than 500 visitors from all over Europe and the United States, with simultaneous translation provided. I was one of three lecturers, along with Albert Hofmann, who was called the "father of LSD," and the prodigious author of a comprehensive encyclopedia of psychedelics, Dr. Christian Rätsch. When my turn to speak came, I spoke about my twenty-five years of research on hallucinogens and culture. My presentation included a discussion of what I was by then calling "drug tourism."

My interest in this phenomenon had started earlier that year, when a woman came to see me at home. She was a friend of a friend of someone I knew in Peru. It was clear that she was in an altered state, and I learned that she had been taking ayahuasca almost daily in Peru until she returned to the United States the previous week. She claimed to be "merging with the universe" (clearly a psychotic state!), and her job, it seemed, was to beat the bushes for American clients for an unscrupulous so-called shaman healer in Peru who had been "treating" people with ayahuasca drinks to promote his "healing" activities. I became determined to expose this misuse of long-held healing traditions by charlatans who had little concern for their clients' well-being.

By this time, I was very aware of the role of suggestibility as part of the psychedelic state and the ease with which such unscrupulous healers could use this property of the substance for their own malevolent and selfish ends. My mention of this subject during my lecture in Göttingen must have hit a nerve among some of the symposium attendees: during the question-and-answer portion of the program, a noted German psychiatrist and concert pianist got up and excoriated that part of my presentation. How dare I mock don so-and-so, who was his beloved ayahuasca healer in Peru! Two years later *Omni Magazine,* which had a very large readership, published my first 750 words bemoaning the phenomenon of drug tourism.

In June 1992, I traveled to Vancouver, British Columbia, as a guest of the psychiatry department of the University of British Columbia. There I gave a series of talks on my work with minority mental-health issues, as well as on my psychedelic studies. The latter was of more interest to the hospital staff in one institution I visited outside of Vancouver.

In 1995 I was invited to the Stanford Health Policy Forum on alternative medicine, where I talked about don Hilde's work in Peru. In October 1997, I presented grand rounds in the cultural psychiatry unit of the University of Miami, where there was interest in the interdisciplinary work I was doing. In October 1999, I helped train docents at the Bowers Museum in Southern California on facets of shamanistic religion in preparation for an exhibit on Panamanian shamanism.

The highlight of this decade was to be my work with the União do Vegetal Church, in Brazil, concerning their conflict with the U.S. government over the issue of sacramental use of ayahuasca in church rituals. Adolescents and children, as well as adults, imbibe the *hoasca* (the Portuguese word for ayahuasca) at least twice a month. In 1997, Yando and I spent time in four Brazilian cities—São Paulo, Rio de Janeiro, Brasilia, and Manaus—and visited some eleven different temples, while living in church members' homes. I observed two ayahuasca sessions in large temples with comfortable seating in São Paulo and Brasilia; music and sermons accompanied the ayahuasca ingestion. We inspected several botanical gardens and hothouses where ayahuasca was cultivated, as well as observing a *preparo,* a ceremony where large amounts of the plant was prepared in industrial-type furnaces for future use.

In 1999 I spent another ten days with Brazilian colleagues in São Paulo, helping to design research with adolescents who had been taking the ayahuasca. This binational team from the United States and Brazil worked really well together. My concern was the qualitative aspect of the research; it was a grueling ten days to work up a protocol for testing forty young members of the União do Vegetal Church and a comparable control group. By 2005 we had all the materials on hand, and Dr. Grob and I would go on to edit an issue of the *Journal of Psychoactive Drugs* on the results of this study.

One group was comprised of the teens from the church who had a history of ayahuasca use twice a month. The second group of teens was a control group who were not members of the church but drawn from the same schools, with no prior history of ayahuasca use. A battery of neurological tests, questionnaires, and vignette commentaries were obtained from both groups. There are few studies with this sort of design in the world of psychedelic research. We rounded out the issue with other biochemical studies and commentaries from scholars doing research on ayahuasca.

6

The Millennium

THE MILLENNIUM SAW AN INTEGRATIVE attempt on my part to deal with lessons learned from shamanic healing in Peru and apply them to techniques that could benefit psychotherapists. In April 2000, I visited some colleagues in Santa Fe, New Mexico, to discuss ayahuasca healing in Peru—the same month that I published a paper, "Lessons from Shamanic Healing," which appeared in the *American Journal of Public Health* and was well received. In fact, the next year, on the basis of that article, I was invited to Chicago to talk at a psychology meeting on spirituality and healing at the Prevention First Conference in Oak Brook, Illinois. In June 2001, I was invited to Scottsdale, Arizona, to give a talk on historical and cross-cultural perspectives on the use of psychoactive substances in spiritual practices. This conference was organized by the National Institute on Drug Abuse, and I spoke to a full auditorium of researchers. Many of them had not heard anything about the phenomenon of drug tourism.

One of my colleagues, psychiatrist Oscar Janiger, who was best known for his LSD research, passed away in 2002, and, along with many other presenters, I gave a eulogy for him at the National History Museum Auditorium in Los Angeles. Our book, *LSD, Spirituality, and the Creative Process,* published in 2003 by Inner Traditions, was based on Janiger's work with 950 men and women from Los Angeles who were given Sandoz LSD in the years 1954–62, long before very much was known about it.

In 2002 I went to London, where the October Gallery hosted an evening talk on my psychedelic research. While in London I also spoke to a full house of interested people about my psychedelic research at the College of Psychic Studies. In February 2003, I gave a talk at UCLA on "LSD, Spirituality, and the Creative Process," hosted by the Council on Spiritual Practices. They had received a grant from the John Templeton Foundation and were very interested in the scientific study of psychedelics. By this time, my book with the late Dr. Janiger had been published, and I participated in some book signings in the Los Angeles area, in Santa Cruz, and San Francisco—always to a full house of interested readers. My talk at the City Lights Bookstore in San Francisco was a highlight of that activity! I continued with my writings on psychedelics, having retired from Cal State Fullerton in January 2000. I presently continue my psychotherapy practice four days a week, in Fullerton, California.

In November 2004, I was invited to the University of California, Santa Barbara, College of Creative Studies, where I talked about psychedelics and tribal arts, again to a full house of both students and teaching staff. That same month I gave my talk on lessons from shamanic healing at a large gathering of the annual meeting of the Latino Behavioral Health Institute, at Universal Studios Hotel.

Interest in psychedelics was on an upsurge by 2006. The previous year the Los Angeles Museum of Contemporary Art had mounted an exhibit called Ecstasy: In and About Altered States, which ran through February 20, 2006. I gave a talk and fielded questions from an audience of several hundred people who came long distances on a rare rainy day in January. I also published a book review on the museum's exhibition catalog in the *Journal of Nervous and Mental Diseases*.

That year in April, I was invited to the Council Grove Conference on Consciousness in Kansas, a small conference of luminaries in the field of consciousness and biofeedback research. There I talked about my experiences with the boa to a general audience interested in consciousness studies. The upshot was that unlike my informants in Belen, who did see the boa whenever they had a good trip with ayahuasca, there was no boa in my life, since snakes and I had little traffic together.

In May 2007, I was invited by Bertrand Hell, an anthropologist whose work focused on the North African trance phenomena, to give a talk, in English, during a forthcoming visit to Paris. The topic was "Urban Shamanism in the Peruvian Amazon," and the venue was the École des hautes études en sciences sociales, where philosophers like Derrida and Foucault had made their mark. The room was full, and after the talk we adjourned to a nearby café for several hours. In the audience was the Peruvian cultural attaché, who suggested I prepare a travel advisory against drug tourism for visitors to Peru, but I declined to do so, thinking that was their job, not mine.

Later that year Yando and I went back to Peru. This was the first visit I had made since 1979, and the population appeared to have doubled in Lima, Iquitos, and Pucallpa. When we visited the market above Belen, we could hardly find the Amazon River because there were many concrete buildings several stories high that had not been there years before blocking the view. In Lima, I gave a talk in Spanish at a large private university, the Universidad Alas Perúanas, or UAP, which had recently published my talk on drug tourism, the União do Vegetal Church, and tribal use of ayahuasca.

I was pleased that I could disseminate my research to Peruvian scholars who may not have had access to English publications. Most of the young students who filled the hall knew very little about ayahuasca in their own country and even less about the phenomenon of drug tourism. The following week I gave a similar talk at the Institute of Amazonian Studies (Instituto de Investigaciones del Amazonía Perúana) in Iquitos. This was a scientific group mainly concerned with botanical research and the maintenance of botanical gardens. My colleague and longtime friend Roger Rumrrill, a Peruvian writer and journalist, interviewed several shamans for a new book that we were finishing together. Rumrrill arranged interviews with some twenty-seven different healers at all levels, from indigenous shamans in the faraway river systems, rural and urban farmers, and mestizo healers, to many of the new urban shamans. That afternoon in Iquitos we spent time with one Shipibo Indian healer, don Guillermo. His healing center, named after the anaconda—

A Shipibo home and its owner outside of Pucallpa, Peru.

mother spirit of the vine—was an oasis of tranquillity after the bustle of the noisy city of Iquitos. The food in the jungle was wonderful.

With this decade coming to a close, I could see a certain slowing down of my schedule. The book on drug tourism that Roger and I wrote, *A Hallucinogenic Tea, Laced with Controversy,* was published in 2008, and I today continue my work with art and psychedelics, encouraging young scholars around the world to prepare their studies for dissemination. Recent work with the União do Vegetal Church points out the important role of ayahuasca as a sacrament in religious arenas. The decision by the United States Supreme Court to permit the use the plant in the U.S. branch of the União do Vegetal Church has certainly made history.

PART TWO

■ ■ ■

PSYCHEDELIC
RESEARCH SUMMARIES

■ ■ ■ ■ ■ ■ ■ ■

AFTER ALMOST FORTY-FIVE YEARS of observing other people ingest psychedelics and of studying, either in person or through books and articles,
the monumental architecture and ancient artifacts of long-gone cultures
that used psychedelics, I find it worthwhile to stop and reflect on the
lessons I have learned in my research on the anthropology of psychedelics. My work has touched on a number of distinctive areas: cultural
evolutionary process, symbolic behavior, psychiatry and psychology, ethnobotany, art history, music and theater, ethnography, and parapsychology. Of interest as well is my interdisciplinary research with Brazilian
and American scientists on the adolescents of the União do Vegetal
Church and, more recently, with the excesses of drug tourism.

Hallucinogens have always been viewed in human cultures as a
double-edged sword. On the one hand, they have been used by different societies over time and space because of their perceived ability
to allow people to access spiritual realms. The idea here is that if we
change our body chemistry, we can enter realms of being that most
ordinary human beings do not have access to. Other scientists see this
as faulty wiring and argue that plant chemicals deceive and trick us.
In the Euroamerican world of rationality, access to the spirit realm is
not possible, and all we have left are tricks of the mind. Still others see
plant hallucinogens as a tool or a psychotechnology that allows tribal
elders to manage the altered states of consciousness of their adolescents
through hypersuggestibility to brainwash their youth in the service of
survival.

CULTURAL EVOLUTIONARY PROCESS

Those anthropologists who work within the paradigm of cultural evolution look at the vast array of human societies in terms of historical
changes, from simple to more complex. Culture is seen as a way to
help human beings adapt to distinctive ecological niches of the planet.
Anthropologists value individual societies that can survive in hostile
environments, and they study the particular adaptations they must
make to do so.

Over the course of history, societies have moved in the direction
of more complexity. The model that I like to work with examines different types of societies, from hunter-gatherers to incipient agricultur-
alists, intensive farmers, and state-level societies such as the pristine
states that developed historically: the Maya, the Aztec, the Inca, the
Mesopotamians, the Chinese, and the Northern India-Pakistanis. In
this model we find that as societies become more complex, psychedelic
use also changes. Access to substance-induced altered states of consciousness becomes regulated by laws put in place by elites, as fewer and fewer
individual members of society are permitted entry into those altered
states. Substance use, under these circumstances, may even become a
crime against the commonwealth.

These plants, believed to confer power on the user, which that
person could then use to control others, to bewitch an enemy, and to
even cause death, could be dangerous to elites. However, this contrasts
with the reality of psychedelic use among hunter-gatherers, illustrated
in one society in 1973 by anthropologist Janet Siskind: among eighty
people who lived in a Peruvian rain forest, as many as twenty-five adult
men used ayahuasca in ritual ceremonies twice a week or more, so as to
become of "one heart" and to better share resources and cooperate with
each other.

Rituals, then, changed over time—from exoteric ones, open
and accessible to all adults and adolescents, to esoteric, secret rituals
like the Eleusinian Mysteries in ancient Greece, which the amateur

ethnomycologist Gordon Wasson and his colleagues wrote about in 1977 in *The Road to Eleusis: Unveiling the Secret of the Mysteries.*

In state-level society, if a peasant shaman was permitted to use hallucinogenic plants, and if beliefs existed that such a person could bewitch a state administrator, legitimate power would be seen to be in jeopardy. Once higher-ranking groups of people usurped control of hallucinogens, the quick demise of knowledge of these substances is predictable, especially if change in cultures occurs in the form of conquest, colonialism, or bureaucratization. At that point, esoteric knowledge does not again diffuse down to the folk level, from where it surely originated. As fewer and fewer people are involved in the hallucinogenic experience, many of the beliefs connected to such psychedelic use became encoded in the religious art of these societies. With social change, these belief systems disappeared, and such knowledge could only be retrieved in contemporary times through an analysis of the art of those societies.

In the pages to come, my research since 1967 will be summarized in terms of a series of themes. After many years of research it is difficult to do this in a succinct format, and certainly I will try hard not to repeat myself as different perspectives on the cultural use of psychedelics are presented. Two major themes are highlighted. The first is the refusal of Western scholars to acknowledge the important role of plant psychedelics in human history and expressive behavior. Even when we have hard evidence of biochemical knowledge, and even when there is independent verification, for instance from missionaries, learned priests, or world travelers who recorded psychedelic rituals, scholars often skim over the indications of the impact and importance of such historical and contemporary use.

The second area I wish to highlight is the enormous potential of these plants to create hypersuggestible states that can be used to manage others and that can be used to socialize young people into their proper roles as emerging adults, thus contributing to the long-term survival of the cultural group. There surely must be lessons here for postindustrial societies like our own.

In the following pages, I will highlight the seven areas of my research on psychedelics. They are: theoretical approaches; ethnographies of tribal and ancient civilizations' use of plant psychedelics; reinterpreting the archaeological record; psychedelics and healing; psychedelics, art, music; ayahuasca as a sacrament in the União do Vegetal Church of Brazil; and drug tourism in the Amazon. These research areas stem from the many books and articles I have published since my early years in Salas and Belen, Peru. At the end of this book, I will look at the direction that my psychedelic research may take in the future.

7

Theoretical Approaches to Psychedelic Research

WHEN I BEGAN TO CONDUCT research on psychedelics and culture, there was a real lack of general knowledge about and documentation of the use of these substances, especially in tribal and Third World cultures. What information did exist was scattered and in hard-to-find academic journals and books. In this chapter I summarize some of my findings and examine the role of the shaman in healing and in providing security to his fellows by means of psychedelic ritual. Such an overview of hallucinogens in these societies teaches us how psychedelics have been used to inculcate beliefs, expectations, and values, allowing us to predict the effects of the substances and understand the role of set and setting—that is, what the individual brings to the hallucinogenic experience in terms of his expectations, beliefs, and values, and the set or environment in which the experience occurs—in a quiet nature setting or a loud nightclub dance milieu.

We see how hallucinogenic rituals, despite legal constraints to control the ingestion of plant hallucinogens, nevertheless occur worldwide. Terminology is very important, and the field of psychedelic research has been plagued by problems of nomenclature. A new term, *entheogen*, is examined for its possible use or rejection. Women have played a secondary role historically in managing psychedelic states, and I examine this phenomenon in terms of the biological constraints that have limited women's participation in psychedelic rituals until they reach menopause.

MAN, CULTURE, AND HALLUCINOGENS

Anthropologists pride themselves on their ability to create theory in the social sciences. Studying the use of plant hallucinogens in tribal societies allows us to understand states of mind and how different cultures around the world have been able to harness the power of psychedelics to avoid dependency on and abuse of these plants. As a result of my cross-cultural research on plant psychedelics, I have come to recognize the important role of culture and how it structures the psychedelic experience.

From a Western perspective, the idea that visionary experience is culturally patterned appears as something of an anomaly. Mostly, reports of visionary states are idiosyncratic. People reared in societies in which visionary plants have been used traditionally, however, enter their experience with certain expectations about the content and form of their visions. In other words, culture determines the stereotyping of hallucinatory visions.

The plant psychedelic itself is not responsible for the ensuing pharmacologic effects. Rather, these are mediated by the setting and set (as discussed earlier) and other factors, such as the belief systems, expectations, and values connected to the plant's use. Scientists call these "antecedent variables." In turn, these interact with the pharmacological properties of the plant so as to help us predict the effects of the psychedelic.

Anthropologists work in a natural laboratory, whereas shamans use psychedelics ritually. The scientist cannot control nor at times adequately measure such elements as somatic effects, reduced intellectual-motor proficiency, changes in visual perceptions, and other effects in the mind or body in any kind of rigorous manner. However, by looking at the antecedent variables, the scientist can arrive at reasonable conclusions that contribute to the overall body of knowledge. For instance, the anthropologist can focus on the group of beliefs that surround a society's use of hallucinogens; on the cognitive system that deals with the belief in the power of the plant; and on its visionary content, especially when these plants are used for healing, witchcraft, or in religious activity. The shared expectations of members of the community give rise to the expectation that certain visions will arise, and in fact these very visions are reported with frequency.

Anthropologists understand that people are born into a society and become socialized in the lifestyles that are part and parcel of that culture. They acquire expectations about the preternatural, about how the hallucinogen will open portals to the sacred. They display these social characteristics when they enter into altered states of consciousness. Antecedents include biological, psychological, social-interactional, and cultural variables. The body weight, physical condition, special diets, and sexual abstinence all contribute to the outcome of the psychedelic experience. The person's motivation to take the substance, his attitudes, personality, mood, and past experiences all influence the outcome as well. Typically such substances are taken in a group, and group dynamics, leadership roles, rivalries, ritual performances, and the presence of a guide also have to be factored in. Finally, from a cultural perspective, both the shaman and the client share the same symbolic system, beliefs, and values: they expect a certain visionary content, and they are subject to the same nonverbal adjuncts, such as music and pleasant odors.

Many of these antecedent variables are not considered by those researching the use of these substances in Western society. However, tribal society has been able to harness the effects of these plants for goals that benefit the society, specifically because of their concern for the *entire* context in which they are used.

The boa, once again, is important to this discussion. If you grow up in the Bronx, a cement jungle, chances are that you would know little if anything about the boa, the mother spirit of the ayahuasca plant. It certainly would not be valued or expected as visionary content resulting from ingesting the jungle tea. It certainly is not a part of the everyday chatter of our world. No boa in the Bronx!

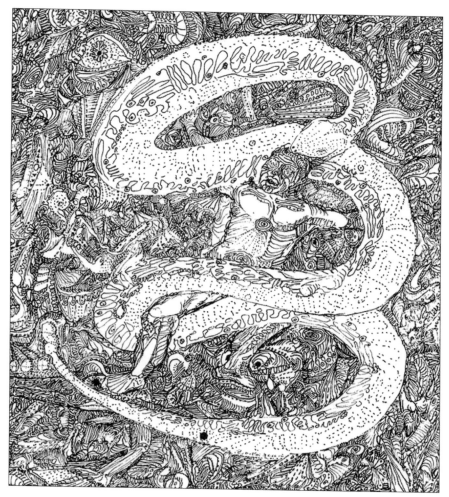

A black-and-white drawing of the boa. Artwork courtesy of Yando Rios.

SHAMANISM,
ONTOLOGY, AND HUMAN EVOLUTION

As more and more ethnographic material comes to light, we begin to understand how important the shamanic healer has historically been to human well-being and to the evolutionary success of the species. Most physical anthropologists will tell you at great length how puny and lacking in power *Homo sapiens* were in the course of their evolution when they faced much more fierce competitors in the animal kingdom. The branch of philosophy known as ontology—the study of the nature of reality—helps us understand the key values of the shaman: namely, the search for power and control over nature and over his fellow man.

Shamans all over the world, including the Amazon, have been needed to control nature, spirits, and animals on behalf of their societies. In traditional cultures, hunting and gathering were the main ways that people survived. In such an environment there were many implicit and explicit dangers—threats from predators, predictable shortfalls in food, and lack of shelter. Under the circumstances, people could easily experience a state of helplessness, hopelessness, and despair, which could lead to a disinclination to respond actively to the challenges of life: one just gives up. In psychological terms, this would be classified as a major depressive episode with melancholic features, according to *The Diagnostic and Statistical Manual of Mental Disorders*.

If, however, members of a community collectively believed that their shaman or shamans, having been properly trained and apprenticed, had links to supernatural spirits through the use of plant hallucinogens, this would affirm their belief in the shaman's ability to exercise power and control over nature and make the spirit forces of plants or animals act bountifully on their behalf. This would create the phenomenon known as the biology of hope, mentioned earlier in conjunction with healing rituals employing ayahuasca. So when we look at how healing occurs, we see that a person's negative emotional state can exacerbate the threats to their survival. When people feel helpless, hopeless, and at a loss due to the stressors in their environment, depression can easily develop. People slow down, become agitated, and lose weight. Their immune system becomes compromised, making them more susceptible to disease.

The traditional role of the shaman, then, is to reverse such negative emotions by cutting short the feeling of helplessness and making life psychologically more secure and satisfying. This ability of the shaman to empower the individuals within his society is indeed a vitally important psychotechnology. On the physical level this can bring about a positive immunological response, thus enabling individuals within the collective to be successful in the face of a difficult and often hostile environment and contributing to the evolutionary success of their society.

In addition, by being able to call on the qualities of nature spirits, the shaman is also a true leader and protector of the commonwealth. Called a "corruption of reality," people culturally construct their own world because too much reality can be a problem. Some atheists would argue that illusion and self-deception serve to help human beings survive through their religious beliefs, which may propose spiritual beings that can be called upon to do a shaman's bidding on behalf of the community. The plant hallucinogens in the environment can often give one the feeling that one's body is changing into another form—shape-shifting into that of an animal, for example. This strengthens the belief in the shaman's control over animal familiars and tutelary spirits as he shifts his own shape into those creatures to heighten his personal power in the service of the community.

THE FUNCTION OF DRUG RITUALS IN HUMAN SOCIETY

There was a real interest in rituals connected to psychedelic ingestion during the 1970s. Ubiquitous in the long history of humankind's use of psychedelics is the continuity of the ritualization of such substances when used socially.

Rituals are stylized, and prescribed behaviors surround the ingestion of a psychedelic. The methods to procure and administer the hallucinogen, the selection of the physical and social setting for use, the activities after the psychedelic is administered, and the methods of preventing untoward aftereffects are all in place. There are also norms that determine how or whether a particular substance should be used, with informal and often unspoken values or rules of conduct shared by the social group.

We can gain insights into continuities and changes in the use of psychoactive substances throughout human history by drawing on anthropological theory. Cross-cultural definitions of ritual help us to understand how the use of psychedelics does not bring about negative results. Such rituals in human societies serve a multitude of purposes. Ritual is an established or prescribed procedure for a religious or other formal or ceremonial act or procedure. Most psychedelic ingestion in traditional societies occurs in a context of sacred meaning. Rituals occur when human beings recognize a "more than human realm" with which they deal repeatedly; most often there is a customary observance or practice involved. A more secular definition of ritual includes any practice or pattern of behavior that is repeated in a prescribed manner. Beliefs and rituals go hand in hand: belief serves to explain, rationalize, interpret, and direct the energy of the ritual performance. The purpose of the ritual is to confer benefits or avert the misfortunes of those for whom the ritual is performed. This is done by means of actions and words that produce a psychological effect on the participants, although the words and actions in themselves could be entirely ineffective.

Some scholars view ritual as being basically psychological in function, an obsessive repetitive action that symbolically dramatizes the fundamental needs of a society. These needs could be economic, biological, social, or sexual. Ritual is enacted to transform human beings psychologically to achieve a desired end state or else to prevent an undesired transformation from occurring. Other rituals try to control human health. Some rituals invoke supernatural beings, while others invoke an impersonal supernatural force or energy, often called power, or mana. Psychedelic users are quick to argue that such substances are therapeutically necessary for their spiritual health in that an expanded consciousness is believed to put a person in touch with universal energies—much like communicating with the divine—thus conferring benefit.

There are many reports that illustrate the use of psychedelics in witchcraft and healing, as well as to cause retribution for supposed wrongdoing by evil men and women. Psychedelic ritual can function as salvation, to enable the person to attain a sense of renewal. (I talk about hallucinogens and redemption in chapter 12, which deals with the União do Vegetal Church and with the use of ayahuasca to assist in addicts' recovery from cocaine, alcohol, methamphetamine, and aggressive lifestyles.)

The person who takes psychedelics in a cultural context often has an intensely gratifying and insightful experience. Sometimes this may happen as a rite of rebellion, when people are required to do the "wrong thing." One of the ultimate goals of social control may be to allow people to let off steam so that order and stability in society can be maintained. Rituals of rebellion allow impulses that are chronically frustrated otherwise to be vented.

In traditional societies of the world, rituals occur periodically throughout the life cycle. Historically, rites of passage, usually at adolescence, directed emerging adults toward the change in their social role and asked that they leave behind their artifacts, their identities, and their names of childhood. Psychedelic plants have often been part of the rituals involved in these liminal stages, when groups of youth are segregated from the larger society and the process of transformation formally occurs.

Rituals are adaptive in human society because they promote social solidarity, whether within a subgroup of the society or in the larger social unit. Émile Durkheim, the father of modern sociology, argued that the function of religious behavior was basically social—to promote the solidarity of the group. Rituals often bring people together in situations where quarreling is forbidden. Another approach to ritual that can be applied to psychedelic ingestion can be found in the work of anthropologist Roy Rappaport, who in 1971 argued that ritual is an information-exchange device that communicates cultural, ecological, and demographic data across the boundaries of local social groups. This information can then be used in planning short-range ecological and social strategies. Rituals are considered to be high-value situations—in other words, sacred. Information accepted by the group is believed to be true, even when there are conflicts.

During ritual activities, people communicate information concerning their physiological, psychological, or sociological states to themselves and to other participants. Because, according to Rappaport, human beings are the only members of the animal kingdom who are able to lie, the general sanctity of the ritual event imbues a quality of unquestionable truthfulness that participants attribute to often unverifiable propositions. This is what lends a sacred quality to ritual. People are likely to accept sanctified messages as true, which makes their behavior predictable. Ritual thus helps a group survive, or at the very least, provides a minimum degree of orderliness in social interactions.

The data that my colleague Dr. David Smith and I published in 1977 shows that in traditional societies of the world, psychedelic rituals developed in place of abuse and legal restrictions on use. With psychedelics thus embedded in group process in these cultures, and with clearly delineated cultural goals and group ingestion within a ritual framework directing the personal experience, there is little room for these people to develop a dependency on hallucinogens. Thus, in traditional societies the problem of abuse rarely occurs.

HALLUCINOGENS:
A CROSS-CULTURAL PERSPECTIVE

My book *Hallucinogens: Cross-cultural Perspectives* had a long development. It started out as a report I prepared in 1973 for the Second National Commission on Marijuana and Drug Abuse and metamorphosed into its most recent form (which was in continuous publication for many years before going out of print). Since the time of its original publication in 1984, drug policy in the United States underwent some major changes with the War on Drugs and the general recognition of runaway abuse of psychoactive substances by large segments of the American population. My goal in writing the book was to document recurrent cross-cultural regularities that one could observe among traditional societies that used psychedelic plants. The societies I included in my book were the Australian Aborigines, the reindeer herdsmen of Siberia, the Plains Indians of North America, the Nazca fishermen of coastal Peru, the New Guinea highlanders, the Moche of Peru, the ancient Maya, the Aztecs of Mexico, the Incas of Peru, the Fang of the northwestern equatorial Africa, and urban Amazonian mestizos of Peru. My summaries of several of these societies' use of hallucinogens will be presented in chapter 8.

My study was an attempt to provide a key to understanding the art of prehistoric peoples and to reveal some of their belief systems, which are generally elusive in the archaeological record. The work also gave us a departure point for comparing ancient use of psychedelics to contemporary use and for looking at drug-abuse issues in our own society. In my research on hallucinogenic plants and culture and my cross-cultural analyses of the symbolic and instrumental uses of such powerful substances, I was able to see how plant hallucinogens are a double-edged sword. From earliest times, human beings have turned to these plants to create nonordinary states of consciousness that allow one to perceive spirit realms said to be omnipresent and accessible.

This was done with a chemical boost in what Charles Grob and I termed "managed altered states of consciousness." In traditional societies such substances were given by elders to their society's adolescents in a fully rational and planned way to create special states of consciousness for them, using the resulting state of heightened suggestibility for the inculcation of cultural values and norms. This contrasts with advanced industrial societies such as Europe and North America, where psychoactive chemicals and, to a lesser degree, plants have been used without any kind of managerial wisdom. The result is that the suggestible states that result from taking these substances come into play by default, in ways that are harmful to youth—which contributes to rampant drug abuse.

Psychoactive-drug use among American adolescents has reached epidemic proportions over the past two to three decades. Despite increasing attention given to this phenomenon by the media and the government as well as health and educational authorities and services, widespread misuse and abuse of drugs and alcohol by the young persists virtually unabated. Today it is statistically normative for adolescents to engage in some degree of illegal drug-taking. In fact, the United States has a more severe and pervasive substance-abuse problem than any other industrialized nation of the world.

When we contrast tribal hallucinogen-use patterns with drug use in societies such as our own, we note that initiation rites in contemporary industrialized societies have fallen by the wayside. Modern life denies us any access to the awareness of the need for renewal. Drug use often becomes a desperate but futile self-medicating attempt at initiation among Western youth.

In *Hallucinogens: Cross-cultural Perspectives,* I saw that hallucinogens have generally been accepted as sacred in origin and treated with awe and reverence. In traditional societies' rites of passage, during which plant hallucinogens are used, the release into initiatory "death" followed by "rebirth" is a recurrent theme. The life of the child/adolescent in these societies undergoes sharp changes as the youth succeeds in obtaining a new identity that is richly imbued with meaning and meriting societal respect and attention.

In Western society we lack initiatory and transitional rites and traditions. The synthetic, manufactured drugs available are recognized as a major problem that contemporary society must contend with. The sacred and reverent use of psychoactive substances among tribal peoples is transformed by Western industrial societies into the profane and pathological phenomenon that we define as drug abuse. As we learn more about the anthropological record of plant-psychedelic use, this knowledge may better equip us to address the tragedy of contemporary drug abuse.

ENTHEOGENS: A NEW TERMINOLOGY

Religious thinkers from the Council on Spiritual Practices, Harvard University, and the Chicago Theological Seminary came together in 1992 to rethink the terminology that has been used to describe that class of plants called psychedelics or hallucinogens. In a response to an article in the *Journal of Psychoactive Drugs* that examined this new term that has become so popular in the media in recent years, I took issue with the etymology and meanings that were being attributed to it. The term, *entheogen*, has as its main root the Greek word *theo*—God—and translates as "creates God within."

This group of scholars appears to have overlooked the anthropological perspective and disregarded non-Western traditional society perspectives. In fact, there is a real ethnocentric bias in the theological perspective evident in this coinage. *Homo sapiens* have been on the face of the earth for several million years in one form or other. Cultural evolutionists have generally accepted the fact that there are four major types of religious systems that characterize human prehistory. The first, that of shamanism, is the religion of the hunter-gatherers and has been around for 99.9 percent of human prehistory. This has given way to communal, polytheistic, and monotheistic systems only since the advent of agriculture, no earlier than 12,000 years before the present.

As a result of this typology, we can easily trace the theological orientation of *Homo sapiens*. Early times appear to have given rise to human hominids who focused on spirits of animals, plants, and natural phenomena, as well as on celestial bodies. With the advent of agriculture this came to include sacred aspects of nature, ancestor worship, and human spiritual forms, which over time became divine forms. Then we see named gods and goddesses, and finally a superordinate force, generally viewed as a single, monotheistic God.

This progression has hardly been unilineal. Throughout the world, we find multiple religious systems within any nation-state. It is totally inaccurate to talk about God as if this were the natural form of worship over time, when indeed such a concept of a sole supernatural being represents religious perceptions that characterize less than 1 percent of human history. When native peoples who use plant hallucinogens in tribal societies around the world do so, they generally do it in the context of seeking out exogenous forces—outside of themselves—rather than generating a divine force within the individual or releasing a feeling that is within the person.

Of course, nation-states with monotheistic religious systems dominate world societies today. Nonetheless, we can argue that perhaps as many as 30 to 40 percent of the world's populations have recourse to nontheistic spiritual domains. To foist an ethnocentric and noninformed term on the language is to continue to view the sacred with cultural blinders on.

In my cross-cultural studies of hallucinogens, I found that one of the major themes in religious activity that incorporates psychedelics is the use of the word *power,* as compared with the notion of supplicating a single divine source deemed more powerful than human beings. There are several religious activities of a syncretistic nature, in which Christian elements have been blended with native belief systems—the Native American Church's use of peyote, for example, to facilitate communion with Jesus. However, most of the world's populations did not, and many do not, use such psychoactive substances to communicate with God, as suggested by those who loosely use the term *entheology.* It is time that scholars of different persuasions begin to read one another's work so that they can, at least, recognize the boundaries that require respect.

Michael Winkelman, an anthropologist, has offered us the term *psychointegrator* to emphasize the positive aspects of this class of substances—certainly a more neutral term than *entheogen.* Winkelman's term "reflects the substances' systemic neuro-phenomenological effects, integrating brain processes and experiences." The word *psychedelic* has been around for more than fifty years, while the word *hallucinogen* is more likely to be found in scientific studies. I interchange *psychedelic* and *hallucinogen* throughout this book and try to avoid the word *drug,* with its strong negative connotations, unless I am referring to tourism with these substances, which has greater affinity to narcotics trafficking.

WOMEN AND HALLUCINOGENS

The question about women's role in the history of plant-psychedelic use in society is a fascinating topic. These plants have been used as facilitators for religious ecstasy and to allow people to enter into direct contact with spirit or divinity. In most of human prehistory they are associated with nomadic hunter-gatherer societies in which women did not hunt, and as the result of their lower social status they were relegated to the private domain of the hearth.

In an early paper I wrote that women were excluded from the hunt because of the odors associated with menstrual blood, lactation, and other reproductive olfactory intrusions. Hence they were kept away from hunting implements and often made to obey strict taboos during the time of their menses. Ingestion of psychedelic plants by women in prehistoric periods was quite incidental and not seen to be an appropriate activity for women.

When we look at evidence from contemporary hunting and gathering societies, we see that once a woman reaches menopause, the nonordinary state of consciousness that could be obtained by intoxicants and hallucinogens would occur more frequently. With the domestication of plants and animals about 10,000 to 12,000 years ago, there were some changes in the use of hallucinogens. For example, contemporary African societies such as the Tsogana Tsonga of Mozambique use *Datura fatuosa* in girls' schools to promote fertility. They do this by cueing the young women to have a culturally stereotyped vision of the god, a blue snake, that they believe ensures fertility. In the Peruvian Amazon, women seek out traditional healers known to employ powerful psychedelics such as ayahuasca. Both the healer and client experience a visionary state to help them identify any witchcraft that might be responsible for the woman's illness or misfortune. Overall, though, plant hallucinogens in these settings are taken in rituals, and mostly by men.

Women in the Amazon rain forest often seek hallucinogenic visions to solve personal and marital problems, but they play a minor role in ritual performances and as ayahuasca healers. This is changing with the neoshamans and as the result of drug tourism (which I delve into later in this book). In recent research that Roger Rumrrill and I published in 2007, only three out of twenty-seven shamans we interviewed were women. These women were relatively young and in their prime of life, and they paid little heed to proscriptions around menstruation and ayahuasca access. However, their services were marketed to tourists, not local people. In this latter case, there was a worldview that forbade women from entering the forest or going in a boat on the river when they were having their periods.

In recent years, few pregnant women in Peru are invited to take part in ayahuasca rituals due to the substance's purgative effects and the fear that diarrhea and vomiting might provoke premature labor. However, in the Brazilian church União do Vegetal, where ayahuasca is used as a sacrament, women are given a small amount of a tea made from ayahuasca during their pregnancy and labor to enhance their health, without any apparent dangerous side effects reported.

In New Guinea, among the Kuma peoples of the Mt. Hagen region, there is a totally different pattern of women's use of hallucinogens, which was studied by an Australian anthropologist Marie Reay in the 1960s. Both men and women ingested wild mushrooms as condiments. Once a year, a combative frenzy was caused by these plants. The women chased up and down the mountain in a dance formation; they whistled, sang, giggled, and laughed; they let out loud yells and experienced an intoxication that lasted several days. Some become delirious and irresponsible. Women became boastful of real or imagined sexual adventures, and sometimes they were so embarrassed by their own behavior that they plunged into a nearby river to try to stop the hallucinations while the men stood by and watched from a distance.

Overall, research based on my own work and that of other scholars shows that women's role in hallucinogenic ritual performance is minimal. In shamanic cultures one doesn't achieve any goals of salvation, and the chief focus is on power and its exercise by religious practitioners, who are mainly men. Only after menopause, while in a liminal state, did women transcend the gender limitations imposed on them by their culture and have access to psychoactive substances, and only in a limited fashion at that.

8

Psychedelics
and
Ethnographies

TO REMEDY THE LACK OF centralized ethnographies on cultures in which hallucinogens have been in use over the years, I gathered information from diverse sources in several languages that I could read, first as part of my report for the Second National Commission on Marihuana and Drug Abuse, and subsequently for my book *Hallucinogens: Cross-cultural Perspectives.*

In this section, I summarize the ways in which psychedelic plants have been used by the Australian Aborigines, the New Guinean herders, the Fang of northwestern equatorial Africa, the Aztecs, the Incas, and the villagers and healers of Salas, Peru. I also include summaries of two articles that Charles Grob and I published on adolescent ingestion of hallucinogens during rites of passage conducted by the Chumash of central California, the Tsogana Tsonga of Mozambique, and the Australian Aborigines. Tobacco, not generally considered to be a hallucinogen, indeed may very well be one. I comment on an important research project on tobacco use among tribal societies of South America and link the findings to my work in the Amazon, since tobacco is a companion plant, in the form of secondary smoke, to the ayahuasca potions given by healers and shamans.

AUSTRALIAN ABORIGINES

During the summer of 1970, when I was a visiting scientist at the Smithsonian Institution in Washington, D.C., I had occasion to view a good deal of tribal art as I worked on my report for the museum on tribal use of plant psychedelics. I came across information on the Australian Aborigines' use of plant hallucinogens, particularly pituri (*Duboisia hopwoodii*), in their hunter-gatherer culture, whose traditional lifestyle largely came to an end in the early part of the twentieth century as these native peoples acculturated.

When the Europeans came to Australia in 1788, and Dutch explorers reached the northern and western coasts of the continent, there were some 500 tribes of Aborigines who were seminomadic. These tribal groups typically included anywhere from 100 to 500 people, and they used thirteen different species of native wild tobacco as well as pituri. Small doses of pituri, which contains the psychedelic alkaloids scopolamine and hyoscamine, give rise to hallucinations and illusions and a sense of detachment from time and space. This plant was important in the social life of the Aborigines.

Like other psychedelics used around the world, the plant could quell hunger and thirst and make life tolerable in the desert. It enabled Aborigines to travel long distances in search of the basic necessities of life. There were pituri roads—extensive trade networks that extended from the northern to the southern reaches of the desert area. The plant was widely traded for items such as spears, boomerangs, nets, shields, fish, and yams. The pituri roads crossed rivers and high mountain ranges. Pituri leaves were packed tightly into woven bags and traded over hundreds of miles. The plant was given as a token of friendship to strangers and used as a pick-me-up and social comforter to foster feelings of friendship. It was placed in small water holes as bait to trap emus, parrots, and kangaroos. Native people chewed the plant in their interactions with one another. Old men, who acted as seers, consumed the plant to obtain power and riches.

The Aborigines also practiced painful genital cuttings on their young men in rites of passage at puberty; records show that the plant was used in payment for these circumcisions and subincisions and as an anesthesia. In the subincision procedure, the urethra of the penis was cut with an obsidian blade and thereafter men had to urinate in a squatting position. There was periodic bleeding from the incision. While scopolamine did not actually eliminate pain, its soporific properties helped the person forget such a surgical experience. In fact, scopolamine was used after World War II in the United States for women undergoing labor and was affectionately called "twilight sleep"—this author was born under this medicine in 1939. Psychoanalysts have had a field day discussing the symbolism of female envy and fecundity issues, but we have no way to assume this connection was made by the Aborigines.

While the Aborigines did not have a writing system per se, they did have incised wooden message sticks that were used by tribal groups to indicate to other neighboring tribes that they wanted to trade the plant. A complex sign language grew up around pituri. Old men sent message sticks to the owner of the commodity—similar to the use of a king's signet ring in medieval days to show the legitimacy of the king from whom the request was made. A messenger who carried these special insignia would indicate what quantity of the plant he desired. These sticks were memory devices, as the notches and marks of different kinds were cut into the wood as aids in helping the messengers recall their cargo. The sticks also functioned as safe conduct in hostile territory. Ritual activities were connected to the acacia bush, the wirra, which was added to the pituri mixture, just as ash is added to the coca leaf in highland Peru today to release its alkaloid properties.

When the Europeans introduced processed tobacco cigarettes, pituri use disappeared. As a result, many of the traditional customs of the Aborigines no longer exist. Today, many Native people have moved to reservations set aside for them or are assimilated into Western lifestyles, making the pituri plant but a dim memory. Though the use of this plant was shrouded in secrecy, we do know it was vital in capturing the emu, whose meat was one of the main sources of animal protein available to Aborigines. The emus would be lured to water holes that had been laced with the plant. They would become intoxicated and easy to catch, hence one of the other names for pituri, emu plant.

From our ability to reconstruct the use of this plant among the Aborigines, it is likely that the plant impressed the Aboriginal shaman and his initiate as a vehicle of communication with the supernatural world. The plant may have been used to induce trance and for other divinatory purposes as well; we know that the Aboriginal word for *trance* disappeared from their language around the same time that the pituri plant fell into disuse.

Moreover, pituri served as a revered totemic plant in Aborigine society. In totemic belief, an animal or a natural object would be considered ancestrally related to a kinship group and taken as its symbol; it would be held in high regard. The full use of pituri, however, remains a subject of speculation.

NEW GUINEA MUSHROOM USERS

In the highlands of western New Guinea, agricultural and herding peoples called the Kuma and Kaimbi have used plant psychedelics differently from other tribal groups around the world. The plants that are used include the wild mushrooms of the *Boletus* and *Psilocybe* genera. These psychedelics are used in a mundane, secular fashion. And unlike other societies that I have studied in which plant psychedelics are used to establish a relationship between tribal peoples and the supernatural, the Kuma and Kaimbi use them to resolve tension and conflict within their community.

The Kuma depend on horticulture: they raise sweet potatoes, bananas, maize, beans, and sugarcane. They also herd pigs, which provide them with their main source of protein. Mostly men are involved in everyday activities, which are oriented toward self-aggrandizement and the accumulation and display of wealth, measured by the possession of pigs. Men wish to triumph over others and become a "big man" as a primary goal in this society.

As far back as 1947, an anthropologist wrote about the use of a wild mushroom, locally called nonda (*Boletus manicus*), which excited the tribespeople into a combative frenzy and made users temporarily insane. The plant was also ingested before going out to kill others in warfare, and during times of great excitement, anger, or sorrow, before the Australian colonizers brought an end to tribal warfare.

In 1961, two scholars, the French mycologist Roger Heim and the amateur ethnomycologist Gordon Wasson, visited New Guinea for a few weeks and attempted to identify and collect nonda mushrooms. It is interesting to note that although the Kuma eat the mushroom mixed with other vegetables throughout the year, it is only in the dry season that people experience the "mushroom madness." The French mycologist actually identified a new species of psilosybin, called *Psilocybe kumaenorum,* similar to the Mexican variety, which contains alkaloids.

The boletus contains traces of the LSD-like substance psilocybin. Missionary reports describe an occasion when six young men under the influence of the mushrooms rushed about chasing people, threatening them with spears after they ate what were described as toadstools or poisonous mushrooms. The plant caused blurred vision and made people deaf and crazy as they ran up and down the mountain. This display of limitless energy occurred in both men and women.

When the women were involved in such activities, they became delirious and irresponsible. They danced, whistled and sang, giggled and laughed, and let out loud yells. This behavior lasted for a couple of days. They had their husbands or sons decorate them in their best feathers. They were given weapons to hold. The married women then danced in formation in the way that men and unmarried girls do. When the women returned to their houses, they boasted of real or imaginary sexual adventures. Sometimes women who felt an attack coming on would plunge into a nearby river to try to halt the temporary insanity.

When men were under the influence of the plant, they put on all kinds of ornaments, took up their weapons, and ran about terrorizing everyone in sight. They even attacked their clansmen and families, although few people suffered from any serious wounds from their badly aimed arrows. They were described as tense and excited; they reported seeing double and suffering from aphasia, impervious to the demands of those around them.

The peak periods of this mushroom madness are in late May and early June. Both the Kuma and Kaimbi define the madness as temporary insanity. However, in recent years this temporary madness has never led to death. Villagers deliberately encourage the men to be aggressive. Women who dress like men and behave like transvestites symbolize the alteration of their traditional low status in society. This has been called a rite of rebellion—not unlike the American folk event known as Sadie Hawkins Day.

One early study found that 10 percent of one New Guinea community became seized by the madness (however, children do not participate in these rituals). For the most part, the tribespeople unanimously report that these mushrooms cause negative effects—a bad trip. They exhibit fear of their hallucinations, fear of hurting someone, fear of having to be subdued by one's kinfolk, and terrible fright at the thought of having to spend the night alone in the bush. Nonetheless, this running-amok behavior is a kind of institutionalized deviance that allows people at certain times of stress to channel antisocial sentiments into a limited range of activities. There is no penalty or stigma for misbehaving in ways that are normally forbidden. This madness thus periodically allows for the socially sanctioned expression of antisocial behavior.

THE FANG OF
NORTHWESTERN EQUATORIAL AFRICA

The Fang, in northwestern equatorial Africa, live in the present-day Democratic Republic of the Congo (formerly Zaire). This is a place with high temperatures and humidity, heavy rainfall, and dense forests. Farming peanuts, corn, manioc, and plantains, these agricultural and commerce-oriented people were under European colonial rule for at least a hundred years. Under French domination, many aboriginal life patterns changed, and social upheavals resulted.

The hallucinogenic plant *Tabernanthe iboga* has been incorporated into a religious revitalization movement known as the Bwiti cult, which started around the time of the First World War, and perhaps even as early as 1863. Only about 10 percent of the Fang people are involved in the Bwiti movement. The colonial situation caused many frustrations in French-speaking Africa. Some Bantu rituals in central Gabon were borrowed and incorporated into the cult. Most of our knowledge about the connection between this plant and Bwiti has been contributed by two scientists—the French sociologist, anthropologist, and ethnologist Georges Balandier and the American anthropologist James Fernandez.

The cult grew from 1920 to 1930 and spread across Cameroon in West Africa. French colonial and missionary opposition to Bwiti occurred around 1931, and some temples were destroyed; thereafter the movement became clandestine. After the Second World War, the Bwiti villages tended to concentrate in marginal areas. The cult blends elements of traditional Fang beliefs with Christian symbols. In recent years, the cult honors particular ancestors and conducts rites linked to fertility (fertility assurances being very important to members of the cult), and helps to cement feelings of group solidarity.

In villages that are involved with the cult, the Bwiti temple occupies a position of privilege. Animal sacrifices are made when a new temple is founded, and the sacrifice symbolizes a break with normal kinship ties. Bwiti temples are quite large and impressive. In each temple there is a central post covered with carved figures and symbols that express the personality of different groups. Some of the symbols have male sexual motifs; others have intricately sculpted female genitalia and breasts. These latter types of carvings represent the principal female divinity—a "first woman"—who is a link between the earth and the sky. A third type of post symbolism, found in the more Westernized villages, incorporates Christian iconography. Balandier viewed the cult as presenting its members with a cosmogony of religious thoughts centered on the idea of fecundity and death, as well as a defense against the dangers of sorcery. With social disorganization, individual competition, and changing social conditions, more sorcery has been occurring in the tribe, causing conflict in these communities.

In the Democratic Republic of the Congo and surrounding areas such as Gabon, Angola, and Cameroon, the iboga shrub—three or four feet in height—grows wild. In Europe scholars knew this plant to be a powerful stimulant and aphrodisiac. Fang hunters find it an excellent way to keep themselves constantly awake during night watches while hunting for game, and they praise the plant's ability to eliminate fatigue. Large dosages of iboga bring on fantastic visions, convulsions, and paralysis, as well as the occasional death. Some Gabonese informants have reported that the plant's effects are identical to alcohol, although it does not disturb thought processes. Smaller amounts of the plant produce marginal hallucinatory effects and possibly a dreamy or floating sensation.

Like other psychedelics, iboga allows people to go for days without sleeping. It was said that the Fang learned about the properties of the plant by observing boars, porcupines, and gorillas. Boars in particular were said to dig up and eat the roots of the plant and go into a wild frenzy, jumping around in fright from their visions. By eating the iboga plant in cult rituals, a person sees the Bwiti, a superior divinity. Members of the movement, which is mainly male but has a sister sect, drink a concoction made from the gratings of the plant's root.

Iboga is generally consumed first by tribal members at their Bwiti initiation, after they paint their bodies white and red, which are symbols of good and evil. Initiates dress in tiger skins, part of the warrior's traditional costume. These costumes are resplendent and stimulate perceptual changes when a person is under the psychedelic effects of the plant. Tribal members believe that the plant offers revelations and power, revealed knowledge being highly valued by the Fang, who consider it a separate reality from everyday life. Most, if not all, initiates claim to see this power, whether real or imagined. Fang traditional culture focuses on the worship of ancestors, who play an important role in directing the lives of those still on earth. Under the influence of iboga, the Bwiti initiates are able to communicate directly with an assembly of dead ones—a chain of ancestors.

The initiate falls to the ground in a stupor after drinking the iboga brew. The Bwiti then is supposed to reveal itself under diverse and macabre forms. One report details a Bwiti vision that features a disembodied eye in a grotesque dance. Under the influence of the iboga, the person sees a phantasm, who takes him by the hand and conducts him around 1,000 turns and detours to a place with one hut and one door. The door is opened, and the initiate sees a long procession of skeletons and cadavers representing ancestors pass in front of his eyes—pale, gesticulating, and giving off an insufferable odor. The initiate then sees the Bwiti divinity—before the vision disappears. Afterward, members of the inner circle interrogate the new candidate to determine if his vision is sufficiently appropriate so that he can be admitted to the cult. If the person does not see the Bwiti, he is given repeated doses of iboga, which may kill him and his doubts. Fernandez reported a dozen cases over the past forty years in which initiates died from suspected overdoses.

The typical visions reported by Fernandez show the curing of an illness, or an initiate is said to walk over a long, multicolored road, or over many rivers leading to the place of one's ancestors. Through their intervention, the initiate meets the great gods. Genealogies are very important, since they reaffirm man's relationship to his ancestors. This explains the columns of dead people in iboga visions, which are legendary genealogical frameworks. After these nightlong rituals with iboga, cult members report that they achieve a state of one-heartedness. During initiation, when the members are engaged in the search for deep contact with Bwiti, they ingest the plant. Bwiti cult members may also take iboga several times during their lifetime.

The Bwiti cult has established order in a society in which ancient systems of social control have been eroded and where colonial conditions have dehumanized people. For the Fang, the psychedelic helps people adapt from a state of social instability characterized by the colonial period to one of cohesive well-being. The Bwiti gives these kinship groups a sanctified character by incorporating the iboga plant into its rituals, because it permits people to have direct communication with the valued ancestors of the past.

THE AZTECS OF MEXICO

The Aztecs were an ancient urban civilization based on irrigation agriculture. They gained control over neighboring territory prior to the arrival of the Spanish in the Americas in the sixteenth century, and their empire was held together by warfare and a system of unsteady alliances and power politics.

The Aztec social system was a stratified one that consisted of a noble class that was not hereditary, a group of priests and high functionaries, and an intermediate group of merchants and entrepreneurs. An enormous peasant class tilled the soil and was occupied with crafts. Estimates of pre-Columbian populations range as high as ten million, comparable to the civilizations of ancient Egypt and Babylonia. Upon their arrival, the Spanish encountered fine cities and broad avenues, stepped pyramids, monumental sculpture, and sumptuous residential palaces certainly equal to such grandeur on their own continent.

Four different hallucinogenic drugs were ingested by the Aztecs not only to communicate with the supernatural but also as an important part of their war-related activities and as part of their human sacrifices. Plant hallucinogens also played an important role in facilitating political alliances between the great states that made up the confederated Aztec Empire. A special priesthood was in control of the hallucinogenic plants. The Aztecs viewed themselves as the people of the Sun. Warfare was devoted to capturing human beings, whom they sacrificed to their bloodthirsty deity. Hallucinogens were used to lighten the pain of captives and to make them oblivious to their fate.

The Aztecs used peyote, a small, spineless cactus that contains various alkaloids, including mescaline. The intoxication lasted from two to three days, and those who ate the plant were said to see visions that either frightened them or made them laugh—the heavens or hells often reported from other psychedelic experiences. It is probable that the Aztecs learned about peyote from other northern groups called Mexicas during the period when the Aztecs were a nomadic and barbarian culture, as far back as 300 BCE. Peyote was transported several hundred miles to the Valley of Mexico in a dried state. The Spanish missionary Bernardino de Sahagún suggested that peyote gave the Aztecs the courage to fight and to be free from fear, hunger, and thirst.

Hallucinogenic mushrooms, members of the *Stropharia* and *Psilocybe* genera, were called teonanácatl, or flesh of the gods, and were another important part of Aztec ritual life. An early writer documented the costliness of these mushrooms and the all-night vigils required to find them. They were eaten raw and caused people to have strange hallucinations and vivid dreams. As reported to the Spanish missionaries, the altered states included hilarity, excitation, "demonic" visions, torpor, and feelings of well-being. Some reported that they saw snakes and other frightening things.

A third category of hallucinogens, toloache, from the *Datura* genus, was valued for the drowsiness it created. Toloache was used for healing and as a local anesthetic.

The fourth favorite plant was the morning glory, called oliloqui (*Ipomoea violacea*). The vision-inducing, lentil-like seeds from this vine were esteemed as a divine messenger that transported people to spiritual realms. Those who ate the seeds were believed to be deprived of their reason.

The Aztecs were a polytheistic people. There was a large class of priests and priestesses that specialized in the cults of the gods. They performed rites and ceremonies to propitiate these forces. The power

of plant hallucinogens was believed to bestow on the taker the ability
to summon spiritual forces to one's aid. The person who imbibed a
sacred plant would become possessed of its powers and could control
the spirit of the plant for good or evil. Thus its use by priestly groups
was to discern witchcraft and cure illness. The plants could also be used
to cause harm to one's enemies. In 1502, during the coronation feast
of Montezuma, the divine mushroom was incorporated into the celebration: after war captives were slaughtered in great numbers to honor
Montezuma's accession to the throne, their flesh was eaten and everyone was given raw mushrooms. One Spanish missionary, writing about
this occasion, said that people went out of their minds, in a worse state
than if they had drunk a great quantity of wine. Many took their own
lives. The missionary thought the devil was speaking to them.

Montezuma invited rival rulers to feasts he held three times a year.
Both the invited dignitaries and Montezuma would eat wild mushrooms. Sacred mushrooms played such an important role in Aztec life
that Indian groups who owed tribute to the Aztec emperor paid it in
the form of inebriating mushrooms. The Spanish missionaries believed
that for the Aztecs, the sacred mushrooms were like the host in the
Catholic religion. In this way, they received their god in a form of Holy
Communion but they equated the mushrooms with the devil. In none
of the numerous historical documents I have consulted was there ever
any indication that the priests ingested any of these hallucinogens.

The divinatory powers of hallucinogenic plants, allowing the user to
have the power of second sight and prophecy, were their most important
aspect for the Aztec priests. One could also discover the identity of a
thief, find stolen objects, or predict the outcome of war or the attack of
a hostile group through their use. Sorcerers were said to use the plants
to harm people whom they didn't like. The use of psychedelic mushrooms solemnized occasions and cemented bonds of friendship between
potential enemies.

The Spanish missionaries persecuted priests and practitioners
who used the sacred plants in religious rituals, believing that the devil

himself was involved. While the Aztecs viewed the plants as divine messengers capable of transporting people into spiritual realms, the Spanish saw these plants as impeding on their own missionary activities. The Catholic Church based communion with the supernatural not on a person's revealed knowledge, but in membership in a complex hierarchical structure as well as faith in the church's doctrines. In this context, a person's relationship with the spiritual world could only be mediated by the church's priests. Mysticism, even within the context of Christianity, was (and is still) viewed with suspicion. The basic magical assumption inherent in hallucinogenic use—that human beings are capable of controlling the unknown and can use sacred plants to obtain power that can then be used for good or evil—was totally contrary to Christian concepts. Supplication and submission to God's will characterized European religions, not power and control.

The Spanish colonizers were thorough in their destruction of the hallucinogenic cults. As a result, these practices went underground. Clearly, the descendants of the Aztecs kept their knowledge of the sacred and magical plants hidden from the conquerors for four centuries, until it came to light only in the twentieth century.

THE INCAS

Travel in the Peruvian highlands allows a visitor to marvel at the massive earthworks and archaeological remains of the famous Inca Empire, which existed during the same period as the Aztecs. Although plant hallucinogens and stimulants played an important role in Incan culture, one has to search the record for far-flung data on the psychedelic plants used for religious and healing purposes by this ancient civilization; that is because for the Incas, plant hallucinogens served to a lesser extent than did similar plants in other cultures, as a bridge to the supernatural to aid in diagnosing and treating illness. Not quite as committed to plant hallucinogens, the ancient Incas nonetheless took full advantage of the psychedelic plants in their milieu for healing, witchcraft, and divination.

The Incas had little time to consolidate their newly won empire before the Spanish arrived in the Americas in 1519. The achievements of the Incas centered around their great organizational skills in erecting one of the most cohesive and well-integrated theocratic empires in the history of humankind. They reached an urban level of great sophistication and had a complex transportation system that joined their highland capital, Cuzco, to the entire Andean region—the famous network of highways of the Incas. Estimates of the size of the Incan population were ten million people or more at the time of the Spanish conquest.

Canal irrigation and aqueducts with dikes for water control enhanced agriculture. The Incas took full advantage of guano manure from coastal islands and they used this bird excreta to fertilize their farmlands. In this way they were able to accumulate and distribute large food surpluses to their population so that few people experienced hunger. In addition to agriculture, they raised fur-bearing cameloids such as the llama and alpaca, from whose coats they spun fine wool. Some of the most elaborate textiles ever noted in ancient civilizations were woven by the Incas. Cities numbered in the thousands of inhabitants, with fine temples and palaces. The state was theocratic and highly centralized and was ruled by a hereditary nobility in the sacred person of the Sapa Inca, who was believed to be the son of the Sun. Below the nobility was a stratum of priests and priestesses devoted to a religious cult of the god Viracocha and the sun god Pachacamac, followed by bureaucrats, community headmen, and an urban class of artists, physicians, architects, artisans, and peasantry. The Incas had a large army.

Since the Incas conquered coastal peoples in an area extending several thousand miles from Ecuador to Chile, there is no doubt that their plant list included cultigens in use by earlier groups such as the Moche and Chimu, who flourished from about several hundred years before the time of Christ to approximately 800 CE. We know from my studies of Salas that despite massive cultural changes over the centuries, San Pedro rituals continued with some variations over time.

Certainly at the level of the farmer, it would appear that the San

San Pedro cactus for sale in the Chiclayo market.

Pedro cactus, containing mescaline, had a continuous historical role right up to the present. In addition to the cactus, the coca bush, several varieties of the nightshade family, and the hallucinogenic snuff *Anadenanthera colubrine,* were all important to the Incas.

The coca bush has at least a 2,000-year history in this region. There are ninety species of the plant. The leaves were used for chewing and as a medicine. The end result of chewing coca leaves, depending on the quantity, can be similar in effect to the ingestion of cocaine. The leaves are generally chewed along with a ball of lime, the chemical calcium oxide enhancing the release of its alkaloid properties.

Many coastal archaeological sites point to the early use of coca.

Pottery vessels of the Nazca culture show men with distended cheeks. Dried leaves are found in many Peruvian mummy bundles that date back 2,000 years or more. Coca leaves are represented in metallurgic art, in both gold and silver. Coca was an emblem of the male children of the Incas, a sign of vigor and endurance. The plant was valued for its ability to alleviate thirst and hunger. However, the oldest use of coca was for shamanistic religious practices. The mild mental excitation that follows the chewing of the leaves may have permitted the shaman to easily enter into a trance to communicate with the forces of nature. Coca was considered most sacred, a living manifestation of divinity. Legend has it that the children of the Sun presented the Incas with the coca leaf to satisfy their hunger, to provide the weary with new vigor, and to cause the unhappy to forget their misery. The coca plant also played an important role in maintaining health, as the plant's action enhances the assimilation of other foods, increasing the flow of saliva and gastric secretions while strengthening gastrointestinal muscles.

The Incas restricted the use of coca largely to the nobility and the priesthood, and gifts of the leaf were used as rewards for them. During Incan times, common laborers could not use coca without a license from the Sapa Inca or his governor. The plant was favored by court orators, called *yaravecs*. These were men with excellent memories who could relate the history of their people in detail. They were allowed to chew coca because it was believed that the plant strengthened their memory capacity.

In Cuzco, sacrifices of coca were made. During Incan religious festivals, the leaves were thrown to the four cardinal points or burned on an altar. The plant was used to divine the future before the Sapa Inca undertook important activities. Diviners would chew the leaves and spit the juice into their palms. They extended their two longest fingers and considered the augury as being favorable if the juice ran equally down both fingers and bad if it was unequal in its course.

Along the Incan roads, storehouses contained coca for use by both messengers and troops. Special relay messengers carefully ran along engineered roads in two days' and nights' time to bring fish from the coast up to the mountains, where the Sapa Inca ruler would be in residence. Coca was a valuable asset to this messenger service, providing the endurance needed to complete the task.

Coca trances were involved in witchcraft and medicinal activities. The witches would enter into a sleeplike state to see the people they were poisoning or healing. The Incas hated and feared such practitioners of black magic, and anyone believed guilty of murdering a person by black magic or poison would be killed, along with his entire family.

The Spanish first observed the use of coca in 1533, and from being a substance largely relegated to the elites in Incan society, it quickly spread to the masses and became an economically important plant for the Spanish. The conquerors saw that by giving coca to Indians forced to work in mines and on farms, it enabled them to put in very long hours with little food or water. Sometimes they paid off their Indian slave labor entirely in coca leaves. Today coca is found universally throughout the Peruvian and Bolivian Andes and through much of Colombia, mainly in the highland communities.

Finally, a little known hallucinogenic snuff called wilka (prepared from the *Anadenanthera peregrina* tree), which contains DMT, was also used by the Incas. It was believed that sorcerers were able to communicate with their gods through the visions they had after they mixed wilka seeds in their beer. Missionary reports existed of amateur diviners and fortune-tellers who spoke with the devil by drinking the juice of the seeds in a tea. The evidence shows that wilka use was primarily at the folk level and not incorporated into hieratic religious activities.

SALAS: AN ETHNOGRAPHY

As I have already touched on in chapter 1, Salas is considered the capital of witchcraft. People there are quick to believe that evil airs can produce disease, especially near tombs or ruins of sacred places. Indeed,

The mesa of a healer in Salas, Peru.

this entire region is the home of the ancient pre-Inca societies of the Moche and Chimu. There are hidden pyramids and archaeological sites all throughout the countryside. In the village of Salas, there were few medical facilities; people had a poor diet, and hygienic facilities were few and far between—hence the importance of native healers.

The folk healer's table, or *mesa,* is a powerful portable healing shrine that sits under a tambo. The ritual area is laid out to bewitch as well as to cure. Highly polished and oddly shaped stones, each one of which bears its own name, are laid on the ground. The healer believes that the stones adopt the forms of persons and animals that will attack his clients' enemies. It is said that all of the stones symbolically receive orders from the healer. Defenses against countermagic include a series of highly polished wooden sticks that are stuck in the ground at the head of the table in a protective file, often with carved swords.

Believed to keep evil spirits from approaching, the swords and sticks accompany religious statues and holy pictures such as that of the Virgin of Mercy, the Sacred Heart of Jesus, and other religious icons and crucifixes. There are shards of pottery vessels of the ancient Moche and Chimu eras, called *huacos,* as well. Some are used for love magic when women supplicate the healer to cause a man to become enamored of them. Oddly shaped mineral chunks of fool's gold and silver, believed to confer good luck, adorn the table. Some herbs bottled in liquid are placed on the mesa and prescribed by the healer at the end of the session.

Patients often come from faraway areas of the countryside. A potion is made from the San Pedro cactus, which is cut up into pieces and boiled several hours in a large tin of water until only the essence remains. The San Pedro contains a large amount of mescaline and is often mixed with deadly nightshade plants; it is administered, and the effects last about eight hours. The cactus causes nausea and heavy vomiting, which are welcomed as a way to purge the sick person of impurities.

Around 10 p.m. the ceremony begins under the tambo, with no artificial light provided. A cloth is laid down on the ground; the patients sit alongside of it. The healer and his assistant inhale tobacco and water in the form of a nasal snuff from a shell. The maestro, as the healer is called, sings melodic, lulling songs, some in Spanish and others in Quechua, the language of the Incas that was imposed during the historical colonial times on many non-Incan populations by the Spanish clergy to establish a lingua franca.

From time to time before administering the drink, the healer taps the cup that contains the San Pedro potion against the stones, swords, and polished sticks on the mesa, which is said to enhance its effects. At this point people stand up and leave the tambo to vomit away from the group. Prayers are addressed to the Virgin Mary, Jesus, and God. Each patient, in turn, stands up while the healer removes one of the ornate swords from the earth, places it firmly in the ground between the feet of the sick man or woman, and puts the patient's hands on the handle. Then the assistant rubs the patient's body with the sword as the former stands with arms outstretched in the form of a cross. After all the patients are treated in this manner, the healer spends some private time with each patient to discuss their symptoms and problems. Finally, the songs are resumed, and the assistants sprinkle water in the air and cut the air with the sword to drive out evil spirits. At dawn, the last series of songs are sung and the ceremony is over.

The healers maintain that by remaining under the continuing influence of the cactus themselves, they can obtain insights into the type of illnesses that affect their patients. Their visions, stimulated by the striking of ritual stones and the sparks that fly off them, are a source of pride to the healers and give them a focus concerning which herbs to prescribe. Sometime a small guinea pig is passed over the body of the sick person, a symbolic act that is believed to extract the illness. The animal is subsequently killed and its internal organs are examined to discover where in the patient's body the illness has struck.

Besides some of the ritual objects that are laid out on the mesa, there are Roman Catholic influences in the ritual itself. Many of the postures and movements are lifted intact from church services. Latin prayers, somewhat garbled but still familiar to the villagers in a country that has been predominantly Catholic, are also recited. Catholic saints are supplicated to intercede on behalf of the patients.

At the time of my research, little was known about plant-hallucinogenic ritual healing such as what I witnessed in Salas. Subsequent studies by other researchers were published in the academic literature, but many focused on one particular healer trained in a Catholic seminary who charged very high fees and had a largely tourist clientele.

The healer don Hilde in his consultation office surrounded by medicines and plant infusions.

An Amazon scene.

Don Hilde taking the pulse of a patient in his consultation office.

A painting of a traditional healer with a client. (Courtesy of the artist Eduardo Mesa)

Don Hilde's clinic in Pucallpa, Peru.

Don Hilde in his backyard preparing plant medicine for a client. On the upper right are two bottles of ayahuasca tea for a ceremony.

The author administering a questionnaire to one of don Hilde's patients.

A peasant farmer in a Pucallpa slum hulling rice.

Don Hilde on the outskirts of Pucallpa cutting down a plant to use in remedies for his clients.

An unknown mestizo healer
preparing ayahuasca tea.

Don Hilde with plant
cuttings he will use for
his patients' remedies.

Plant infusions being
prepared by don Hilde
for his patients.

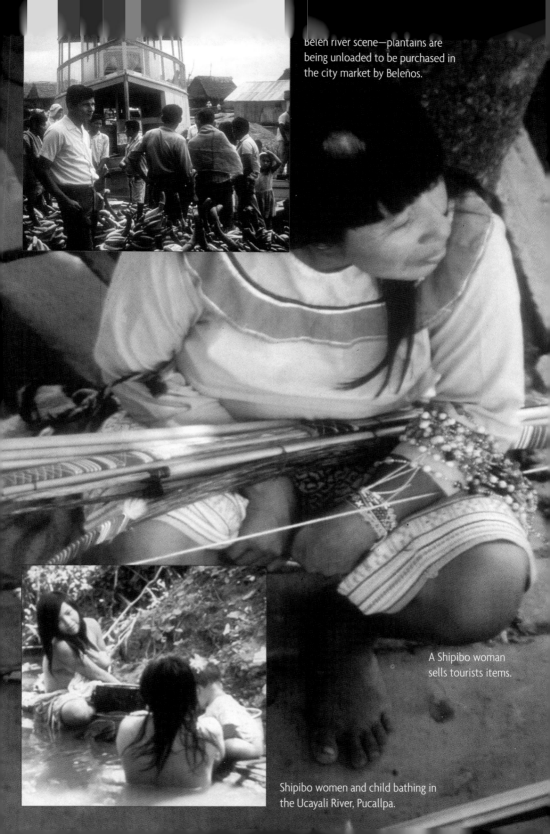

Belén river scene—plantains are being unloaded to be purchased in the city market by Beleños.

A Shipibo woman sells tourists items.

Shipibo women and child bathing in the Ucayali River, Pucallpa.

A street scene in Belen—the raft laden with market produce.

The preparation of ayahuasca tea in a União do Vegetal temple in São Paolo.

A Belen house in the process of being built.

This painting of a flying jaguar, by Yando Rios, depicts the importance of the jaguar among indigenous populations of the Amazon. The jaguar represents a shaman transformed, who is causing an eclipse by covering the sun and the moon with his paws. Oil on canvas, 1971. (Courtesy of the artist Yando Rios)

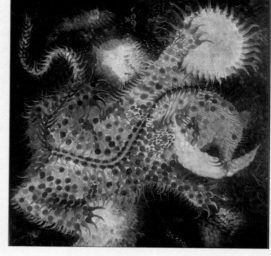

A Moche ceramic showing the shape-shifting of a shaman into an animal familiar, the jaguar.

Iquitos landscape, Peru. Oil on canvas, 1971. (Courtesy of the artist Yando Rios)

Yacumama, the serpent believed to be the mother spirit of the ayahuasca vine. Mixed media, 1999. (Courtesy of the artist Yando Rios)

A depiction of an ayahuasca experience. Oil on canvas, 1970. (Courtesy of the artist Yando Rios)

Another depiction of an ayahuasca experience. Acrylic on canvas, 1990. (Courtesy of the artist Yando Rios)

ADOLESCENT DRUG USE FROM
A CROSS-CULTURAL PERSPECTIVE

In the 1990s, Charles Grob and I collaborated on research that was stimulated by a class of his that I attended, for residents and fellows in the psychiatry department at the UC Irvine Medical Center. As Dr. Grob pointed out particular trends in American adolescent drug use and abuse to the students, I brought up data on one or another tribal society I had studied or taught about, in which plant psychedelics were not used serendipitously but rather were given to young people by elders as part of a fast-paced socialization process that was highly valued in their society. Dr. Grob and I published a paper on the Australian Aborigines, the Tsogana Tsonga, and the Chumash youth. The patterns of psychedelic ingestion in these cultures that we described differed enormously in comparison to the abusive patterns found among American adolescents.

We delineated the concept of managed altered states of consciousness in tribal societies as being situations in which plant hallucinogens were given by elders to their youth as part of an intensive, short-term socialization process for religious and pedagogical purposes. These cultures clearly understood the importance of hypersuggestibility and used these plants as a technique to normalize youth—which is in stark contrast to the pathology of drug use among American adolescents. In the tribal societies, plant-psychedelic use was not problematic, but rather part of a transitional ritual that marked the passage into adulthood, in which adolescent boys and girls were transformed into truly participating members of adult society. Also significant is the distinction between the legal constraints on drug use in Euroamerican society and the absence of such constraints in the ritual use of hallucinogens in traditional societies of the world.

The psychologist Phillip Cushman has written about values in American society in 1990, wherein self-contained individualism is unquestioned. The concept of the self is a bounded, masterful one, unchangeable over time. But Cushman saw the self as empty and lacking meaning. Since World War II, the loss of family, community, and tradition has impacted the self, which is now filled up by consuming goods, calories, romantic partners—and drugs. It seems that people have a compulsion to fill the void with chemically induced experiences. At the same time there is an absence of personal meaning and a hunger for spiritual guidance. The means to do so, however, are not always there for Westerners.

We contrasted the Western pattern of adolescent drug use with the three societies mentioned above. Details of Aboriginal use of pituri have been presented in the previous section on Australian Aborigines. Pituri (*Duboisia hopwoodii*) was used by Aboriginal youth. Scopolamine and hyoscamine—alkaloids in the plant—give rise to hallucinations and illusions and are highly valued among these hunting-and-gathering people for the plant's ability to quiet hunger and quench thirst.

Among the Chumash in the Santa Barbara, California, area, the vision quest at adolescence is linked to the powerful hallucinogenic substance *Datura meteloides,* commonly known as datura, jimsonweed, or toloache (similar to the Spanish word *toloatzin*). Datura use probably diffused northward as a result of Aztec trade and became incorporated into a common pubertal custom of austerities to mark the passage of youth into adulthood. The plant's psychedelic visions were believed to confer knowledge of the future or to make supernatural beings visible to the imbiber. Paranormal events such as clairvoyance were also associated with the plant.

The function of the vision quest is to allow the young Chumash men and women to obtain a supernatural helper or guardian spirit. Datura is integrated into a larger ceremonial complex in which initiates undertake ordeals and learn esoteric lore. The hallucinogenic plant enables contact with the supernatural. Powerful animal familiars teach the initiate a song or dance. The animal then becomes the lifelong totem or guardian spirit/ helper of the youth, believed to be essential to later success as a hunter, shaman, or in any other activity in which that person becomes engaged.

Each youth has an individual sponsor who instructs them in the religious lore of the tribe and teaches him or her various sacred songs and dances. The use of datura tends to be a once-only activity, perhaps due to the difficulty in controlling the effects of the plant. Along with the rituals are purifications, abstinence from sex, and a special diet that forbids salt, fats, and sweets. The dosage level is a key issue in differentiating between a toxic or lethal dose and one simply sufficient to provide the response of a spirit helper.

The last group that Dr. Grob and I considered were the Tsogana Tsonga of Mozambique, which were studied by a graduate student of mine, Thomas Johnston, who lived among this group from 1968 to 1970. They are a patrilineal society that worships the spirits of their ancestors, and they grow maize and other vegetables and keep goats and cattle. Their environment is quite arid, and horticulture is hazardous. Infertility and infant mortality rates are very high due to out-migration of men to cities and mines, where they pick up sexually transmitted diseases. A barren woman can expect a lifetime of disgrace and servitude to others.

A fertility school for nubile adolescent girls is mandatory and takes place each year when the hallucinogenic plant *Datura fatuosa* is given to induce visions of a fertility god, a blue snake. This ritual emphasizes the newly acquired adult status of female initiates and their possibility for motherhood. There are sexual rituals that mimic conception, pregnancy, and childbirth. The girls drink a mixture of the datura and other herbs. Novices are expected to see the culturally expected fertility god, believed to be an ancestor god, and to hear its voice—all of which is simulated largely by the suggestions of the officiant, who psychologically manipulates the novices to ensure group conformity during the rituals. Hypersuggestibility is used, and a group social identity is established, with all the rituals directed toward pride in group membership. The belief is that after ingesting the datura in this puberty-school ritual, the women will be fertile and protected against barrenness, which is believed to be caused by witchcraft. At the end of the school the women are eligible to marry and bring cattle to their fathers in the form of bride wealth.

In all three of these societies, hallucinogenic plants are used to create special states of hypersuggestibility that facilitate the enculturation of adolescent members of the tribe. While under the influence of these substances, learning is heightened and a bond is forged among members of the group, such that individual psychological needs are subsumed by the needs of the collective in order to ensure the survival of the society—a type of aboriginal "boot camp." The hallucinogens create amnesiac states, heightening the symbolic death of the child and his or her rebirth as a contributing adult member of society. In this way of inculcating conformity, group survival and harmony are enhanced. So while in modern Western culture we lack access to adolescent rituals, in tribal societies these rituals are collective and shared experiences. Facilitating individual growth and development allows the society to benefit from the sacred experiences of its youth.

HALLUCINOGENS, SUGGESTIBILITY, AND ADOLESCENCE FROM A CROSS-CULTURAL PERSPECTIVE

When Dr. Grob and I looked at plant hallucinogens among the Aborigine, Chumash, and Tsogana Tsonga tribal societies, we realized that there was more to be said. We saw a sharp distinction between the often irreverent and dangerous use of plant psychedelics in contemporary Western society, and the ritualized, sacrosanct, socially accepted context in which they are taken by tribal peoples, whose aim in their use is to contribute to greater group cohesiveness and to help the youth identify with their society, thus enhancing the survival of the individual and the group. Because of these differences, we decided to focus on the concept of suggestibility as a psychological characteristic of the altered states of consciousness that occur with hallucinogenic ingestion (as well as being a normal human psychological phenomena).

The past forty years, in particular, have seen dysfunctional patterns of family life and radical changes in Western society, in part due to the destabilization of the family structure as a result of the divorce rate in the United States being as high as 67 percent. As a result, the lack of any salutary role on the part of adults in young people's lives has become a critical factor in the undeniably damaging consequences of a good deal of psychedelic use today.

When we examined adolescent drug use in Europe and the United States, we saw that drug-induced states of suggestibility were not managed by Western society's "elders"—that is, parents or other adult figures—as they were by tribal societies' elders. Instead, when young Western people got high—often a form of self-medicating for depression—it was usually part of a complex of suggestibility that included listening to rock music performed by distant, godlike figures (rock stars) whose music often contained antisocial messages. These messages, which deal with values and beliefs, enter the conscious awareness of young people who are under the influence of alcohol, stimulants, marijuana, or psychedelic intoxication. The elevated status of celebrity rock stars, with their enormous influence on youth, magnifies and amplifies such antisocial messages in this theater of suggestibility, which is experienced either in electronic format or in live concerts.

Rock, rap, hip-hop, and video games that young people are exposed to today tend to be preoccupied with themes of violence. There is explicit sexuality and a loss of faith in institutions and authority. Outright hatred and rejection voiced in these mediums reflect the alienation and nihilism of disaffected youth. Songwriters argue that their material is not literal, but rather a parody or just a form of modern "poetry." But adolescents and children as young as eight years of age may not be capable of using operational constructs of an abstract nature to evaluate such music and electronic themes. If children and teens are disturbed, depressed, or under the influence of psychedelics while internalizing messages of suicide, violence, and sexual assault, such pathological thoughts may become legitimized and cause these young people to act on the messages they are hearing. Many emotionally troubled teenagers seen in clinical practice today are alienated and exceptionally vulnerable. They often display desperate, misdirected attempts to connect with something or someone, even if the connection is to a force that emphasizes nihilism, hopelessness, and lack of meaning.

Anthropologists have seen an entirely different pattern in adolescents from tribal cultures. Historically, when these peoples hunted and gathered or engaged in incipient horticulture, tribal elders recognized the value of psychedelic-induced suggestibility and used it constructively within a teaching model to create a sense of conformity to group norms. The potential of hallucinogenic plants to thus enhance the survival of the social polity was clearly recognized, and elders assumed a significant role in managing and regulating the hallucinogenic experience among their young by means of coming-of-age rites.

Suggestibility and Hallucinogens

Some plants among the *Datura* or *Brugmansia* genera have been shown to cause submissive behavior in persons intoxicated with these substances in a shamanic or witchcraft milieu. The person maintains an apparent behavioral integrity but has very severe anterograde amnesia, which interferes with normal memory functioning. The intoxicated person may follow any command and does not present resistance, freely giving money and possessions to the trickster. Psychologist Charles Tart, a leading researcher on consciousness, has written about the increased suggestibility and propensity of a person under the influence of datura to accept or respond to specific statements. Researchers have shown that hallucinogens enhance primary suggestibility to a degree similar to that produced by inducing hypnosis. Indeed, in one major study, mescaline and LSD created trancelike phenomena comparable to hypnosis. Participants in the study experienced intense feelings of detachment or dissociation from their immediate environment and from their sense of self; they became deeply absorbed and felt that their actions and movements were being carried out as though they were asleep; they felt that they were being compelled by a mysterious force; and they also experienced amnesia.

TOBACCO AND SHAMANISM IN SOUTH AMERICA

Since I have written about tobacco as a hallucinogen in my early work with the community of Salas, it is only fitting that I summarize my review of social anthropologist Johannes Wilbert's book *Tobacco and Shamanism in South America,* which deals with the use of tobacco and the shamanism associated with such use among the native peoples throughout the continent.

Anyone who has conducted fieldwork in South American societies in tribal, rural, or urban settings cannot help but note the omnipresent use of tobacco in a variety of forms and modes of ingestion in folk healing, which is commonly associated with hallucinogenic plants. Wilbert has performed a great service to those interested in psychopharmacology, traditional tribal ethnography, and shamanic religion.

In his book, we learn a lot about the ethnobotany and pharmacology of tobacco use in ritual: the author covered three hundred societies, and works published in ten different languages. Tobacco, he concludes, when used ritually by native peoples, reveals pathways to other worlds. Wilbert argues that tobacco may have been the oldest cultigen in the Americas. The first of two major types, *Nicotiana tabacum,* was introduced into South America from the Yucatán in 1535; it is milder in its effect than the far more potent *Nicotiana rustica.*

Native peoples used tobacco for social interactions, warfare, weather control, spiritual concerns, and for healing. There are sixty-seven different methods of internal application of the plant, including chewing, drinking, licking, rectal administration, and snuffing. Smoking is the most common mode of tobacco use in 233 societies, and 133 of these used secondary smoke as adjuncts to healing. Wilbert also presents us with information about snuffing hallucinogenic substances such as *Anadenanthera* sp.

Where plant hallucinogens and tobacco are both available, shamans in traditional tribal societies have historically sought out the substance that would produce the neurological trance experience they wished to obtain. Nicotine, which can create initial tenseness, excitement, rest-lessness, and wakefulness, followed by palpitations, anxiety, fear, and weakness, might be used in frenzy-related activities of an active nature such as rituals related to warfare. Other hallucinogenic plants with different influences on consciousness would be sought after for divinatory or other spiritual activities.

The passive effects of nicotine in healing rituals, where the healer blows smoke over the body and head of a patient, are commonly reported. Long before neuro-imaging technology was available, Wilbert was quick to see that the smoke had positive chemical effects on patients, ranging from stimulation to sedation.

Like many scholars in the area of psychedelics, Wilbert is somewhat reductionistic and views all shamanic activity as a search for chemical effects, neglecting the spiritual concerns of the shaman to communicate with and control spirit forces deemed mighty and powerful. Wilbert also ignores the meaning of the tobacco plant for South American Indians. Beyond his biochemical discussion, he barely hints at the states of consciousness that are accessible with tobacco use or the search for meaning as the basis for such access. Just because it is difficult to measure the search for meaning does not imply that it doesn't exist. Mesoamerican cosmological beliefs suggest that consciousness alterations may have as their goal the discovery of a way to awaken an individual's oneness with the cosmos. Plato stated it best regarding the human need "to step out of the cave of shadows and to find the light of being." Chemical messages in the body need not be viewed as the major, and perhaps only, explanation for the native search for meaning.

9

Psychedelics in
the Archaeological Record

THE ARCHAEOLOGICAL RECORD CAN INFORM us about the importance of plant hallucinogens in ritual and belief, although without any independent verification from other sources we must be careful about the specificity of our suppositions. In this chapter I look at the ritual use of San Pedro in northern coastal Peru and extrapolate back in time to the ancient Moche and Chimu civilizations, which thrived from the time of Christ to around 800 CE, to uncover continuities right up to the present. This is based on my fieldwork in 1967 in Salas.

At the same time that the Moche were active, another prehistoric society, the Nazca, used a variety of plant hallucinogens represented in their textiles, ceramics, and monumental architecture, a subject also discussed in these pages. The ancient Mayan civilization, which flourished from around 2000 BCE to 250 CE, was found to use psychotropic flora and fauna—a discovery that represents a major breakthrough in understanding their beliefs and values.

PSYCHEDELIC FOLK HEALING IN PERU:
CONTINUITY AND CHANGE

An article published in Spanish in 1969 in Peru ("Curanderismo Psicodélico en el Perú: Continuidad y Cambio") examined the use of San Pedro in curing sessions in the village of Salas. My curiosity had been struck by the possibility that this type of healing ritual, with some variations, has had historical continuity over a period of centuries.

True, there were changes that would have occurred as the result of the Spanish conquest; there is even evidence from prehistory that Peruvian rainforest plants and archaeological materials traveled from one region to another. The focus in my research was to establish a line of continuity, from contemporary healing that I observed in Salas in the 1960s to the healing practices of the ancient Moche. My data showed that twentieth-century healers were called on to reverse witchcraft hexes leveled against their clients and to use love magic to enable them to find happiness.

During archaeological periods dating back to around 200 CE, spineless cacti such as the San Pedro variety of the *trichocereus* sps. are represented in the art of the region. During the period of the Moche, the cactus was clearly domesticated, in use, and frequently represented in ceramic art. Moche artists reproduced many figures and scenes of their life and everyday mythology. The San Pedro cactus also was used medicinally. Curative herbs were well established, including purgatives.

Moche ceramics show fruits and plants associated with religious practices. Different illnesses are represented in the art, and healers sucked at the patient's body to remove a foreign substance surely introduced by a witch. This technique of sucking out a foreign element from a patient is very much present throughout Peruvian healing in the Amazon and in isolated areas of the northern Sierras, where San Pedro use occurs. Pieces of cactus in the hands of healers are found in the designs on Moche pottery, and the lack of spines in this cactus makes the San Pedro easy to identify. We also see shape-shifting represented— people being transformed into powerful shamanic familiars or animals. As long as the healers didn't call on Satan in their curing rituals, the Franciscan missionaries allowed them to engage in their healing activities and even allowed them to take the church's sacraments.

Today, many of the rituals employed by the Salas *curanderos* (healers) are blended with Roman Catholic beliefs. There are chapels throughout the region dedicated to the Virgin and to saints, including Saint Cipriano. In ancient times, contact between the northern coast of Peru, a dry, flat desert area, and the Peruvian rain forest would have been difficult but not impossible. Crossing over the high Andes mountain range would have presented challenges. Nonetheless, there appears to be important evidence of cultural contact and commerce between these diverse ecological regions. In fact, similar styles of curing could be argued for San Pedro and ayahuasca rituals, even though a large number of psychedelics used in coastal healing were not readily available in the rainforest habitats. Thus, contact between healers in these early prehistoric periods could be linked to the movement of medicinal plants. The San Pedro cactus grows at 1,500 feet above sea level and has no nutritive value or primary materials, and it lacks thorns that can be used for needles. Its most important property, then, is its psychedelic aspect.

In archaeological museums in Peru we frequently see animals from the Amazon, such as monkeys and parrots, portrayed in the coastal art of antiquity. If the rainforest and coastal peoples were in contact with one another, they would surely share information about their healing flora and fauna. In fact, the lowest peaks of the Andes are found in the northern region, making penetration of the Amazon valleys from the coast feasible. The area of Chachapoyas is the best commercial axis for trade in the highlands. Some ayahuasca seeds from the botanical family to which ayahuasca belongs have been found along the northern coast in an archaeological site. We can't be sure that ayahuasca was used along the coast, but we can assume that an understanding of its psychedelic properties among a sector of the population did exist in this early period.

The Moche drew designs of at least thirty-five different species of birds, sixteen of mammals, and sixteen of fish, condors, pumas, monkeys, and feline creatures in their pottery. The use of the mescaline-containing San Pedro cactus appears to have its roots in antiquity, perhaps as much as 4,000 years before the present time. With the development of pre-Inca agricultural communities along the northern coast and the growth of commerce, these psychedelic substances would have become integrated into the healing arts. Shamans developed specialties to take advantage of this pharmacology, to help deal with the anxieties and uncertainties associated with illness. Thus it would appear that there has been continuous use of San Pedro, probably under different names, as a healing aid for centuries.

Maracas—rattles made of *calaveras,* human skulls—and sounds made from whistling ceramic pots, or *huacos,* may have accompanied ancient psychedelic rituals. Animistic concepts of power appear to have existed in the psychedelic healing substances themselves. The curanderos certainly would have been thought to show their control by the type and number of animal familiars they had available for ritual use. Symbolically extracting the source of illness by rubbing a guinea pig or other objects over the patient's body—same as today—also can be inferred from the art of that period.

We know that throughout history human beings have had to treat endemic illnesses. The psychedelics in these regions became an essential aspect of the treatment. Archaeological data enables us to postulate four stages of healing in the central Andes. The first period, before the development of ceramics, included rituals and propitiation of supernatural forces by shamanic specialists. With the rise of agriculture during a second, pre-ceramic stage, psychedelics began to be incorporated in the paraphernalia and ritual of healing as more knowledge of plants developed. In an intermediate early period, the cause of illness would have been attributed to the supernatural. In the middle to the late periods, a special caste of healers arose who served elite groups. These healing rituals continue today in syncretic form where different religious beliefs and philosophical systems are combined, as we see in Salas today.

PLANT HALLUCINOGENS
AND THE MOCHE RELIGION

After I completed my research on Salas and returned to the States to teach at Cal State Fullerton, I had the opportunity to meet with Douglas Sharon, then a graduate student in anthropology at UCLA, who introduced me to some illustrations of the ceramic art of northern coastal Peru. Peering over books depicting the ceramics of the Moche people, I saw drawings of rituals that were similar to those I had personally observed in the San Pedro ceremonies I chronicled in 1967. I decided to extrapolate from the present, back in time, to hypothesize the way this ancient people used the San Pedro. Not only was the cactus prominently portrayed in the art, but a number of themes emerged that had developed during my work for the Second National Commission on Marijuana and Drug Abuse. At that time, I had prepared a report that later became my second book, *Hallucinogens: Cross-cultural Perspectives*. The themes that emerged from that research could be applied to now-extinct civilizations if we could document that plant hallucinogens were available for use, and if we could find examples of these universal themes in the art of this period.

At the time I conducted research in the 1970s I was surprised at scholars' disinterest in the Moche and their superficial use of data concerning this culture, especially in examining the role, if any, that plant hallucinogens may have played in their religion and rituals. Scholars have been generally disinclined to deal directly with the effects of psychoactive substances as they impacted the belief systems of prehistoric non-Western societies. In my research, I reversed priorities by considering what I saw to be pivotal in traditional Moche life—namely, the use of various plant hallucinogens to achieve contact with supernatural realms and to permit shamans to magically manipulate supernatural forces to serve social goals.

One must be careful not to insist on explicit themes or the delineation of religious beliefs from an analysis of art when no independent verification is available, such as accounts written by Spanish chroniclers of the period. But we can develop a replicable method to interpret the general impact of plant hallucinogens on the religion of various native peoples of the Americas. This summary will focus on the Moche of northern Peru. I will also look at the Maya in Central America. Cross-culturally, there appears to be a finite number of symbols that recur when we extrapolate from contemporary psychedelic-using populations to ancient peoples. The art of different cultures, along with botanical evidence illustrated in the art, allows us to suppose core beliefs that further help us to understand the religions of prehistoric peoples. Moreover, an overview of the art of the Moche shows that this material can best be interpreted as an interplay of complex shamanistic notions of good and evil, power and its manipulation and expression, and the magical control over nature by religious functionaries to serve their clients and community.

Contemporary hallucinogenic use in northern Peru includes the San Pedro cactus, which contains 1.29 grams of mescaline in a given kilo of fresh material. The cactus is cut into small pieces and boiled several hours with *Datura arborea* and two other unidentified plants. Tobacco mixed with water used as a snuff is drawn into the healer's lungs to enhance the potion's effect.

As we saw in Salas, the major use is to treat illnesses that are believed caused by witchcraft. The plant is used as a revelatory agent to make known the source of bewitchment that healer and patient see as being responsible for illness and misfortune. The healing takes place at night in fields distant from houses, under tambos where a healer, his assistant, and patients assemble around a cloth spread out on the ground. These tambos look exactly like the wall-less structures portrayed in the art of the ancient Moche.

When we look at the art of the Moche religion, we see a state society with subsistence based on intensive irrigation agriculture. Large populations exploited both the farming and the maritime realms. There were castlelike fortifications more than a hundred feet high made of many thousands of adobe bricks. The society was probably theocratically organized, with a complex division of labor. Moche society was highly stratified, as reflected in dress, ornament, and temple forms. We see ceramics whose drawings show medicine men performing cures by massaging patients and sucking the affected part of a body to remove a foreign substance, similar to what we still see today; Moche sorcerers carrying in their hands stumps of thornless cacti with a strong likeness to San Pedro; persons transforming into animals in association with a cactus; and depictions of various animals that probably correspond to a shaman's animal familiars.

Themes in Moche art represent a combative shamanistic ethos, reflected in the expansionist, militaristic activities of these peoples. This is unlike the American youthful experiments with psychedelic ingestion during the "peace-and-love" period of the 1960s, which protested the martial activity of the Vietnam War. In the case of the Moche, the use of hallucinogenic plants to access supernatural realms was taking place in the context of that society's expansionism and warfare.

The shaman in Moche life probably had an important role as a protector of seafaring activities. Douglas Sharon observed a San Pedro healer in Trujillo, Peru, who was called on by fishermen to bless a forthcoming expedition with the cactus drink. The theme of shamanic power, as represented in the shaman's transformation into powerful animal figures whom he then sends to do his bidding, to rectify evil or redress harm caused his clients, is a common motif of ceramic art. Often the shaman is depicted as descending to netherworlds to consult with ancestral spirits, or traveling to celestial realms, where he returns with special chants and portents of future happenings.

Among the Moche, the theme of the shaman as warrior is interpreted as shamanistic battling against spirit adversaries. There is armor portrayed, trophy heads, and weapons, which may represent shamanistic protection against evil forces and their defeat. Battle scenes are shown between two people, with the left-sided figure subdued by the one on the right. Symbols of left and right and good and evil are found in the art dealing with global shamanistic activities. There are details of dress and headgear and elaborate buildings where religious activities took place. The nakedness of captured people shows their humiliation. A rope around such a figure's neck may also indicate a two-headed serpent, a familiar of the victorious shaman and not simply a prisoner tied up. It is not likely that the captives represented in the art who are seen with special haircuts represent insanity, mental illness, or fear of being sacrificed; Aztec materials indicate that when war prisoners were sent to their death, they were generally given hallucinogenic mushrooms to make them happy before the sacrifice.

Death haunts all of Moche art. We see the metamorphosis of human beings into animals or plants—a general Pan-American theme. The animal familiars can be seen as being part of a spiritual hierarchy, and not necessarily ordered based on size and ferocity. Just as there are differences among familiars in strength, activity, and power in nature, there are also spiritual hierarchies of individual men. The jaguar or tiger is more powerful than the dog, which is more cunning than the raccoon. The animal familiar has a function to make explicit the relative spiritual power of the shaman.

Another frequent motif is the hummingbird, which symbolizes the aerial voyage when the shaman's animal familiar travels through time and space to carry out his master's bidding. The sucking action of the hummingbird is metaphorically related to the shaman's animal familiar, who sucks at peoples' bodies to withdraw the evil thorn introduced there by a witch. When a person transforms into his familiar, he is shown to be possessed of a powerful spiritual nature represented by the animal or high flyer. The specific animal species defines the social personality of the man vis-à-vis other members of his community.

PLANT HALLUCINOGENS, SEXUALITY, AND THE CERAMIC ART OF THE MOCHE AND NAZCA

One cannot visit the archaeology museums in Peru without noting a profusion of pottery illustrating sexual intercourse and the related activities of the Moche and Nazca cultures in their heyday. These antique ceramics number in the thousands and have been widely exhibited all over the world. The desert coast of Peru is home to this pottery. Sexual representations in the art are always magical and religious in character. Besides a large number of nude figures both male and female, the coastal ceramics show different coital positions, bisexual copulation, fellatio, sodomy, animal-animal copulation; exhibitionism; and childbirth. Ceramics are found with figures displaying exaggerated phalli, and there is great attention paid to anatomical detail.

The Moche had a good sense of humor that has held up across millennia. One pot has an erect phallus presented in exaggerated form as a drinking vessel. To drink liquid from this vessel, one would have to be very careful: To hold the vessel, you would take it by the handle, thus holding the penis in one's hand. Since the neck of the upper portion is full of purposely made holes as the figure's headress, the liquid could spill out. However, the main cavity of the vessel connects to the tip of the penis, so if you didn't want to get wet while drinking, you'd have to drink the liquid through the head of the penis.

This is an area of the world with arid deserts watered by occasional rivers that flow from east to west. There is a richness to the sea, with the cold, nutrient-rich Humboldt Current carrying a large amount of marine life. People in these cultures lived off the sea as fishermen. Great anxiety due to prolonged droughts, alterations in the fertility of fish life in the sea, and the dependence on unpredictable currents is to be inferred. Shamanic themes, for this reason, focus on the control of the environment. There was certainly faith in shamanic leaders, who were believed to have power and control over the reproduction of animal and plant species, as well as control of the environment.

Because the carrying capacity of the region was very fragile, we find no practice that would lead to insemination or subsequent childbirth depicted on Moche pottery. Anal intercourse appears to have been used heterosexually as a form of birth control. Seventeenth-century Catholic priests exhorted their religious converts to extinguish such "ungodly" acts. Yet this sexual custom may have been a mechanism to space births at times when seasonal fluctuations in rainfall, food harvests, availability of fish, and so forth may have been crucial to survival. The archaeological record all over the world is full of evidence of societies that went beyond the carrying capacity of their environment due to overpopulation and subsequently became extinct.

The representation of nude figures in the art that lack genitalia may symbolically represent shamanic and religious persons with a celibacy factor. In cultures in which plant hallucinogens are used, periods of celibacy are generally required of men and women during apprenticeship periods, during which time they live apart from society in wilderness areas while experimenting with numerous plants.

There are a number of ceramics showing a figure seated under a tambo where boiled potions of San Pedro and other hallucinogenic plants are being prepared. An unusual representation is of animated cadavers with erect phalli playing musical instruments similar to panpipes. The figures either kiss or are involved in autoeroticism. Sexual union, death of one's enemy, the spilling of the enemy's blood, and fecundity of the land may be linked and intermingled in these images.

Many of the ceramics that depict sexual themes are of a stirrup-spouted type that can be made to whistle. In contemporary healing activities in Salas, these sounds are said to evoke spirit forces. The ceramics have been linked to shamanic plant-hallucinogen ingestion and are found decorated with designs that represent the healers' animal familiars. In my research, I did not view the illustrations on these pots as the depravity of ancient peoples due to their lascivious and explicit sexual activity, nudity, or exhibitionism, as a Christianized Westerner might.

Instead, my research focused on the *function* of such themes among the ancient Moche and Nazca, particularly the role of plant halluci-nogens used by regional shamanic leaders in facilitating their control over nature—including fecundity of animal species and the fertility of the land and sea. The art probably represented only a small fraction of the total production of religious art but gives us insight into a major theme in pre-Columbian coastal civilizations: namely, the role of pow-erful regional political and religious leaders who try to maintain a bal-ance between the fertility of the resources necessary for survival and the reproductive control of the population.

OUT-OF-BODY EXPERIENCES AND NEW WORLD MONUMENTAL EARTHWORKS

My interest in archaeological monuments and earthworks in cultures in which plant psychedelics were used was heightened by my visits to a number of sites in Peru, particularly among the Nazca ruins, two hours south of Lima. In 1978, my family and I took a wonderful trip to see the famous Nazca lines, a series of geoglyphs in the Nazca Desert, a high arid plateau that stretches more than fifty miles from the town of Nazca. This led me to think about some of the somatic effects of the psychedelics and their influence on the massive earthworks of ancient peoples.

Out-of-body experiences, or the so-called aerial voyage of the sha-man, may have influenced the building of New World massive earth-works. The power of the shaman was made known by the symbols in these earthworks, particularly the animal familiars and cosmological energies that a given shaman could control. Messages about the power of the shaman were made known to all members of the community and reassured individuals that their shaman or shamans were more powerful than those of other communities. This insured survivability in a harsh environment.

The Nazca culture of Peru flourished along the southern desert coast and dates from about 1000 CE. The Nazca are known for some of the finest textiles and ceramics in ancient America. The Nazca Lines, a vast network in the desert plains that has been recorded by scholars, consists of thousands of straight lines so huge that they can only be seen from the height of an airplane. Several hundred such earthworks exist, which were made by removing small stones that covered the desert from the paths. The stones were placed along the sides and form slightly elevated ridges.

This is an area of the world where no rain falls, so that preservation has been fairly continuous. The paths run continuously and never cross, completing the figure close to its beginning. A number of forms can be discerned, including flying birds, insects, felines, killer whales, fish, spiral forms that possibly are coiled snakes, and flying pelicans. Some of these figures are more than 1,700 meters long while others extend over two-and-a-half kilometers. There is no doubt that these are sacred objects. Moreover, all the motifs appearing in the earthworks also occur on the tapestries and ceramics of the region. These figures are always found closely associated with a large enclosure or wide road. Scholars have seen these drawings as a kind of monumental architecture where once important activities occurred. These analyses of the earthworks could only occur after 1944, when aerial photography was employed to map them.

The next step in this puzzle was to establish the presence and availability of plant hallucinogens in the region at this time. North of this area, connected by roads as long as 600 miles, a wide variety of hallucinogenic plants were available, including the San Pedro cactus. This plant was used by the Moche, a people contemporary with the Nazca. The coca plant, also known and chewed throughout Peru, was represented in coastal pottery, and as we have noted it can produce trancelike states in high dosages. Hallucinogenic snuff, from the DMT-containing *Anadenanthera peregrina* bush, is found south and east of the Nazca lines. One can assume that this was incorporated into the culture of the Nazca.

Once we have established that plant hallucinogens were available, we can turn to a commonly reported subjective effect of these plants: the out-of-body experience of the shaman. Such a subjective state can occur spontaneously—without any chemical intervention—and can also take place as part of the psychedelic experience. It has often been called the "depersonalization effect." It includes a wide array of distortions in body image and a schism between body and mind, or dissolution of boundaries between the self and the other, the world, or the universe. The person at times seems to observe objects of perception as if they were not coincident with his physical body. Changes in body images are very common with the ingestion of plant hallucinogens. At high doses bizarre feelings, such as a body melting into the background or floating in space, can register.

In some societies this out-of-body experience is highly valued, especially if the person seeks it through training and repeated efforts. Ranging on a continuum, the effects of an out-of-body experience include such phenomena as seeing one's physical body in objective space but experiencing a no-body-like container that encompasses the external locus of one's awareness. Perception can take on an otherworldly, mystical, paranormal nature.

The famous historian of religion Mircea Eliade has written that shamanistic religion almost always includes the aerial voyage and that shamans fly. This magical power is credited to sorcerers and medicine men. Eliade sees this as purely spiritual in character. To him, flight expresses intelligence, understanding of secret things, or metaphysical truths; magical flight expresses the soul's autonomy and ecstasy. The shaman transcends the human condition, by flying into the air in bird form.

The plant hallucinogens were most likely used to provoke shamanistic out-of-body experiences. Since the shaman is the psychopomp—the spiritual guardian—of his community, he is obliged to confront and combat his group's adversaries. A major part of his activity includes healing disease and neutralizing those misfortunes that have occurred to members of the community through the machinations of enemies. Shamans are able to transform themselves into powerful animal figures whom they send to do their bidding, to rectify evil or redress harm caused to their clients. The effigies of animals and birds found in the massive earthworks of the Americas represent these shamanic familiars. There is a mystical solidarity between humans and animals that is a dominant characteristic of the animistic early religions of these regions. Today we hear about interspecies communication, but that is hardly a new concept!

So the shaman, ingesting psychedelics with spirit familiars on call to serve him, has a subjective component that includes the sensation of flying. My point is quite simple: one need not fly in the air to really fly. Massive earthworks like the Nazca lines, difficult for the Westerner to conceptualize visually outside of an airplane voyage, can be more simply explained as the projection by the shaman of the animal from the heights of ecstasy through which he soars. The geometric forms in the earthworks can be linked to the geometric forms in the kaleidoscopic visionary patterns reported by plant-psychedelic users. These monumental earthworks may have been constructed to warn rival shamans of the powers controlled by the shamans in a given area, to reaffirm supernatural contact, and to maintain social solidarity.

The enormous expenditures of labor and cooperation needed to construct such earthworks, a process that may have extended over generations, reaffirm the bonds that linked people together. The symbolic forms of the image mounds consisted of elements of ritualized beliefs already present in the arts of the culture. These are emblems of power, constructed in the symbolic idiom of each culture, and they give us insight into the area where shamanistic religion and hallucinogenic use converge.

THE MAYA AND THE WATER LILY

In my 1994 study of the ancient Maya, I examined the role of psychedelic flora and fauna in religious rituals. I suggested that the water lily, psilocybin-containing mushrooms, and the bufotenine-containing toad were all part of Mayan religious activities—the water lily in particular being omnipresent in Mayan art. My original article published in 1974 was merely hypothetical, but in 1975 the Mexican biochemist José Luis Diaz found that the water lily in highland Chiapas, Mexico, contained an apomorphine-like alkaloid called aporphine. He used gas-chromatography technology and independently verified my early hypothesis that the water lily was indeed a psychoactive plant.

Aporphine is not a hallucinogen per se, but structurally an opiate. Clinically the chemical has a long history of use in the West as an emetic, causing heavy and continuous vomiting. That would seem inimical to religious experiences such as those sought by Mayan priests to divine the future or to contact supernatural realms. However, once the emetic effect of the plant wears off, a dreamy, languid period follows. Among native societies of the Americas, therapies that included rigorous fasting and vomiting were widely employed by healers to provoke culturally desired altered states of consciousness. The effects of aporphine would be highly valued in that setting.

Several themes emerged from my cross-cultural research on hallucinogens that could be applied to Mayan art. One of these is the Mayan notion of time and how it is perceived: time can slow up to an almost imperceptible flow, or else is experienced as indescribably fast. The Maya have always been associated with a fixation on time, and their monuments chronicle historic events of the period in great detail.

Another widespread theme in the literature on hallucinogens is the role that animals have played in teaching or revealing to human beings the properties of plant hallucinogens. The psychologist Ronald Siegel has shown that animals seek out psychotropic experiences despite their vulnerability to prey species when they are in such states of intoxication. Many societies that used plant hallucinogens have reported learning about such plants from deer, reindeer, or wild boars in their environment. Clearly this points to the antiquity of such plants in human society, because hunter-gatherers going back to the Paleolithic era some 15,000 years ago were probably the first humans to observe the use of these plants by animals, and they then imitated their behavior.

Themes linked to hallucinogenic ingestion can give us insight into the Mayan religion. For example, music as an accompaniment to hallucinogenic plant sessions is important. Healers claim their musical productions evoke certain stereotypic visions, and singing, whistling, or drumming can be viewed as necessary to attain certain cultural goals, such as seeing the person responsible for bewitchment or helping to cure or to foresee the future.

Belen musicians playing different types of melodies.

Another theme of hallucinogenic ingestion is that of the spiritual animation of psychedelic plants. At times these spirit animators are seen to be small to minuscule in size; or they can be gigantic. This kind of visionary experience has been called micropsia or macropsia in the psychiatric literature. For instance, we read reports of the yagé men, named after a common synonym for ayahuasca, small people of the rain forest, or tiny hekula spirits among the Yamamamo Indians of Venezuela, which are tamed by the shaman. The Yanamamo people live in the rain forest in the hills that border Brazil and Venezuela.

Shamanic transformation into animal familiars, aided by a hallucinogenic potion, is another common theme in societies using psychedelics. The shaman is able to control and beckon a series of familiars for his own personal use in curing or bewitching. This concept of binocular rivalry—when one image remains in the mind's eye while a second is superimposed on it, with the first then fading away—is a compelling one. The concept was first brought to my attention in 2008 by Dr. Ede Frecska, a psychiatrist. This may explain the man-to-animal transformation that folklorists call shape-shifting—when the animal's powers are incorporated into the shaman's body.

For a 500-year period, from the middle of the classical Mayan era several hundred years before the common era, the water lily is found to be a very common motif in Mayan art and religious symbolism and is part of a complex of beliefs connected to the maize plant. Death symbols in Mayan art are common, and there are mythic beings seen as the source of the plant, including the long-nosed serpent or rain god, a bird form, and a jaguar. Parts of the body associated with the lily are the top of the head, the ears, eyes, mouth, hands, and the neck and nose regions, which suggest the effects that psychotropic substances have on all the sensory modalities.

At the Mayan ruin of Palenque, in the southern Mexican state of Chiapas, the maize god is found in association with elaborate stems or vines of the lily that pass through his hand. In the famous Dresden Codex, an ancient Mayan book of the eleventh or twelfth century considered the earliest known book of the Americas, the water lily is depicted in the hand of the long-nosed god. Suggestions of paraphernalia are found too, perhaps indicating preparation of the plant, in either a drink or powdered form, to facilitate contact with the supernatural. The lily depicted in the ruins of Copán, in western

Honduras, is associated with the toad, which contains bufotenine and has DMT in its skin. It is shown with its stem emerging from the Copán statue's mouth, and the stalk is held in the hands. Reclining human figures are often placed amid the plants possibly depicting a psychedelic ritual.

10

Psychedelics and Healing

IN RECENT YEARS, PSYCHEDELICS HAVE been reevaluated for their possible role in healing. In this chapter I consider one ayahuasca healer, don Hilde, to see how he incorporated ayahuasca into his mestizo healing techniques and worldview. I pay particular attention to the paranormal abilities attributed to him by his clients in Pucallpa, Peru, and how this aspect of his healing work creates a biology of hope. A culture-specific disorder called *saladera,* new to the psychiatric literature and presenting in 10 percent of don Hilde's adult clients, is described. I also look at the similarities between what Western psychiatric thinking calls paranoia and the belief in witchcraft held by Amazonian patients.

I argue that traditional shamanic healers in the Amazon are astute and have developed very advanced psychological techniques to treat a number of emotional and psychiatric illnesses that their patients report. Recent research on tobacco smoke's emotional benefits explains the important role that such smoke has both in mescaline and ayahuasca healing rituals in Peru. Finally, I look at the powerful hallucinogen ketamine and its use in treating burn victims at the medical facility where I worked for fifteen years.

SOCIOECONOMIC CHARACTERISTICS
OF AN AMAZON URBAN HEALER'S CLIENTELE

To the best of my knowledge, my 1977 study of don Hilde's clients and their experiences with ayahuasca, including the reasons why they drank

Don Hilde bringing home healing plants after a day spent gathering them outside the city of Pucallpa, Peru.

ayahuasca, offered information not generally available to scholars. The research was done while I was on sabbatical from teaching; I spent several months in Pucallpa, living in don Hilde's home. All those who came through his doors were interviewed by me. Most of the patients did not intellectualize the healing process; they simply had faith in the healer and his abilities to help them access other nonhuman realms through his rituals and his knowledge of which plants and drugs and herbs they needed. He was clearly successful, attested to by the frequency of "cured" patients who brought their friends and neighbors to him for treatment. As to his simple lifestyle and low fees, this was not a matter of faith on their part. Healers like don Hilde tend to live a simple lifestyle and charge low fees. This is opposed to the neoshamans we will see in chapter 13 who are out for the tourist buck.

Of particular interest was the way that don Hilde and his patients shared the same world of meaning. Within his community, most of don Hilde's clients believed that illness was caused by the evil of other people. For reasons of envy, revenge, or just plain meanness someone would pay a witch to cause horrendous damage or even death to another person. The main role of the powerful plant hallucinogen ayahuasca was diagnostic and revelatory. During a session, a patient was given the ayahuasca tea to induce visions. That would permit the client to see just what force or which person was believed to be responsible for the evildoing. Only then could the evil magic that caused the illness be deflected or neutralized and cast out by don Hilde. Moreover, it was believed that don Hilde, like certain other ayahuasca healers, had the ability to turn the witchcraft back against the perpetrator—a fitting revenge!

Don Hilde had a history of personal visionary experiences even before he began to work with ayahuasca, when he was in his thirties. His abilities as a visionary probably preempted his depending solely on ayahuasca to produce results. At different times in his life, he pushed ayahuasca to the side, especially in his later years, and worked with his visions alone.

At the time of my study, don Hilde was sixty-three-years-old, a mestizo with only a few years of public-school education. The healer first began to have visions of Christian saints during his adolescence. While in his twenties, he began to heal people in his home while he simultaneously maintained a carpentry shop. After he served in the Peruvian army in the 1930s, he worked as a construction hand to build the Basadre Highway that connected Pucallpa to the coast. Meanwhile, as his reputation as a healer spread, he devoted more time to healing work until it became a full-time activity.

He began to use ayahuasca in the same way that other regional curanderos did. He read about hypnosis and learned to induce trance states in himself. For several years he worked with a mystical order, called Seprionismo de la Amazonía, with spiritualistic influences, and he drew upon the constant, ongoing help of his spirit guide, Inca Man Ko Ka Li, under whose protection he was placed when he joined the group. In all, don Hilde was the heir to a number of traditions: those of Amazonian Indians, Christianity, Masonry, and the nineteenth-century spiritist philosophy of Allan Kardec (the pseudonym of the French teacher and educator Hippolyte Léon Denizard Rivail), which has one of its largest followings in Brazil.

Most healers like don Hilde do not ask questions of their patients. Only apprentices did that. Don Hilde learned to interview his client by means of his own intense concentration as well as pulsing the client. He would pass his hand over the patient's head to read their electro-magnetic energies, and this enabled him to understand whether the illness in question was natural or caused by witchcraft. Further diagnostic insights came from the ayahuasca sessions he conducted three or four times a month in his home in Pucallpa.

Don Hilde learned yogalike breathing exercises from his colleagues at the Septrionic group, and he was able to displace energies in his spiritual healings. The order acknowledges the existence of a father creator, and deity is seen as a conjoint of energies whose mission is to serve humankind. Don Hilde prayed to his spirit guide. He avidly read the Septrionic publications of the founder, whose spiritual name is Shikry Gama, and he listened to cassette tapes brought from Lima to Pucallpa that discussed aspects of the order's doctrines.

Don Hilde grew many medicinal plants in the little garden behind his house, many of which he mixed together with pharmaceutical medicines. They were prepared in accordance with the demands of each case. Periodically he would go to the outskirts of Pucallpa, to a lagoon, where he gathered herbs that he later cooked or seeped in his kitchen while his patients waited in the front room (sala) to be medicated. He added no additional charge for his medicines. Sometimes a difficult case called for in-patient care. Several small rooms were available for that purpose. He referred cases to the hospital when he thought that surgery was indicated.

I interviewed all the patients who came to his clinic on a second visit to Pucallpa in February 1979. I was surprised to find that 71 percent of those interviewed had previously consulted a medical doctor in the city. Both physicians and curanderos are consulted by clients throughout Latin America, generally after modern medicine doesn't solve the problem or its spiritual issues are not viewed as appropriate for Western-type medicine. Fifty-three percent of the patients interviewed were parents of children under seven. Don Hilde didn't charge a set fee for his services but allowed the patient to decide what amount to donate to the healer. He generally received less than 10 percent of the cost of a medical consultation in the city, which was out of the reach of most urban poor.

The question that interested me was whether don Hide and his clients agreed on the illness diagnosis. He recognized two categories of illness: natural and nonnatural. Cultural psychiatrists call this second category culture-specific or culture-bound illness. This category includes *daño* (witchcraft harm to any vulnerable organ of the body) as well as other witchcraft-related illnesses. I found that both don Hilde and his clients would generally concur about the diagnosis of their problems.

Ayahuasca healers like don Hilde saw far more women than men, and the former suffered more illnesses linked to witchcraft. Despite the client's level of education, there was no difference in beliefs held about witchcraft-caused illnesses. Few patients came to see don Hilde for an illness for any extended period of time, and his healing was short term, direct, and crisis oriented.

Witchcraft-related illnesses are believed to be more chronic, and they endure a long time. Only about one-fourth of don Hilde's clients attended his Tuesday-night Septrionic meditation sessions. At the time of my research, it was looking like ayahuasca would die out, as older clients were more familiar with ayahuasca than younger ones. That prediction did not come true as we will see shortly in my discussion of drug tourism. Certainly don Hilde had to pay others to bring the plant from jungle areas farther and farther away from the city. We expected that those under thirty years of age would eventually only know about the substance from reports of their elders. But not so, as we shall see later in chapters 12 and 13, on the União do Vegetal Church and on drug tourism.

I have always been surprised at the willingness of people whom I studied in Peru to discuss their witchcraft fears and experiences with a stranger like myself. Despite rapid culture change, increasing educational access, and mass media, witchcraft beliefs were alive and strong. Age was not important in influencing the type of illness that a patient reported either. For the most part, don Hilde's patients kept silent about their witchcraft fears and were hesitant to make open accusations. Many did not even tell their spouses about their concerns. Those who had strong beliefs in witchcraft had witchcraft-related symptoms that reflected cultural illnesses, and those without strong beliefs in witchcraft showed up with symptoms of natural disorders.

The bottom line was that the rapport between the healer and patient and their shared worldview was the mainstay of the ongoing healing activity in don Hilde's clinic. Later on, when we look at drug tourism, we will see how this powerful belief system about the moral order, good and evil, and the power of witches is totally irrelevant in the lives of the foreign tourists from the United States and Europe who come to the Amazon to take ayahuasca with many of what I refer to as neoshamans—the new breed of so-called healers.

THE VIDENTE PHENOMENON
IN THIRD WORLD TRADITIONAL HEALING

Don Hilde was known as a *vidente*, or seer, and for this reason he was sought after by his clients until his death in 2000. This vidente phenomenon is widespread throughout Latin America; people at all levels of society consult videntes for readings and diagnoses of illnesses. Despite the availability of a Western medical tradition in Amazonian cities, many people still seek out traditional healers who believe they can contact supernatural realms and access divinity to retroactively divulge the origin of illness and ascertain its prognosis. These insights of the healers lead to exceptional emotional responses by the patients. The divinatory insights of healers often occur along with the ingestion of plant psychedelics like ayahuasca. In don Hilde's clinic, both healer and client believe that paranormal phenomena are at work.

The link between paranormal phenomenon and plant hallucinogens, especially the power of these plants to bestow divinatory success, is a near-universal theme in the scientific literature. In fact, when don Hilde used ayahuasca it was mainly to predict the future. In this way the healer was an heir to a tradition going back several thousand years, in which ayahuasca has been used in just such a manner. Amazon Indians used these plants to find out the prognosis of illnesses due to spirit intrusion or witchcraft. Witches tried to capture the spirit forces of powerful plants and animals in their environment and mold them to their own purposes. During the Spanish colonial period, metaphysical beliefs from Europe and the Middle East influenced South American societies.

Thus the rise of the class of people known as videntes is seen everywhere on the continent. The videntes are possessed of supernatural powers and animal familiars, which are used to rectify their clients' interpersonal problems and desire for vengeance. There also developed a class of people called *brujos,* witches, who are renowned for their ability to bewitch others by means of their psychic powers. They are believed able to cause dire illness, misfortune, and even death to their enemies.

By inviting his patient to drink ayahuasca tea along with him, don Hilde's visions might be shared with his client, as he sees whoever is responsible for the bewitchment appearing before him. He would then draw upon his own personal power to nullify the witch's nefarious activities and return the patient to good health. Such a session might require the patient to vomit into a bucket, if needed. This convulsive vomiting occurs about twenty minutes after drinking the tea. People believe that strong vomiting brings a clearer visionary experience. During a session, don Hilde would try to gain as complete an understanding as possible of the cause of a patient's illness, its prognosis, as well as which herbal preparations or pharmaceutical medicines to prescribe.

The ayahuasca visions are considered to be omens of future healing.

From earliest years, the Amazonian resident in cities or small farming villages hears discussions of ayahuasca use. Everyone I met in the Amazon knew at least one adult man or woman who had taken the plant to find out if they were bewitched at the onset of some painful illness. Children generally are present in family and neighborhood discussions concerning ayahuasca, and they acquire many expectations concerning the use of the plant. Adults openly discuss the revelations they had under the influence of ayahuasca while in the presence of their children. Special diets and regimens prescribed by healers will be discussed years after a person's illness has been treated, and the hardships that healers experience during their apprenticeship period, when they live in virgin forest areas with little or no food or salt, earns them the admiration of their urban and rural clients. Some of these healers boast about the time they spent with Indian tribes who taught them secret cures.

Clients of don Hilde admire the ayahuasca potion. The healer's telepathic insights reaffirm the patient's own evaluation of the ill-willed person or brujo whom she believes has bewitched her and who must be faulted for the witchcraft-related illness. Don Hilde is very good at resolving the anxiety his clients experience. His mental abilities are put to use when he prescribes herbs. For example, he visualizes his patient's tumor in the form of round nuclei with many tentacle-like tissues radiating outward in the patient's body. He uses his own mental force, which he projects around the tumor to stop it from spreading.

In interviews with ninety-six patients, all had been referred by a satisfied customer who had already been cured by don Hilde. The referral system sets up an expectation of vidente power before the client even enters the door. Clients would tell me how don Hilde could see the person whom they believed had caused them magical harm or who had paid a witch to make them ill. Not surprisingly, the patient depends on the healer's strength rather than on her own. My anthropological training did not prepare me very well to deal with the paranormal beliefs of my informants in a fieldwork situation.

Don Hilde is part of a historical lineage of shamans. He is not a trickster and has no agents in the community to listen to gossip and report back to him so that, like a nightclub performer, he can startle his client with "magical" mentalist feats. Pucallpa is just too geographically spread out and populated for any trickery of that type to work; people are constantly coming and going, and neighborhoods are reconstituted periodically.

Men and women who leave don Hilde's clinic also leave their anxiety behind. The patient has an unusual psychic encounter and experiences the emotional impact of don Hilde telling it like it is, without asking any questions, and merely describing accurately in the perception of the client the stressors in his personal life. There is absolute anonymity in the clinic: no records, no names, nor is any medical history taken. A sense of intimacy between the healer and patient is created by the force of the paranormal revelations, as both healer and patient share the same assumptive world when dealing with access to spirit forces. Don Hilde is an expert who speaks with authority. Few patients know what preparations he uses or his belief systems. Only the novice asks questions of patients, and don Hilde was definitely not a novice. Intensified emotional states help the body to create biochemicals that dull pain and evoke ecstatic states—the endorphins.

Any cultural belief and activity such as the vidente phenomenon that occurs in urban healing is worth studying. Healers like don Hilde are sought out by patients because of their reputed qualities and abilities as a seer, while on a daily basis the seer reaffirms his abilities in the lives and concerns of his patients through his personal behavior and his integrity.

SALADERA:
A CULTURE-BOUND MISFORTUNE
SYNDROME IN THE PERUVIAN AMAZON

Not enough has been said about the psychological consequences of the rapid acculturation of Third World urbanized peasants, who respond with anxiety and despair to events occurring all around them, over which they seem to have little control. When one is poor, things do go wrong. The culture-bound syndrome saladera, from the Spanish word for salt, *sal*, is commonly treated by Amazonian folk healers like don Hilde. The syndrome is a response to the stress of modernization in a society in which the belief in witchcraft is invoked to explain the etiology of an illness. People who came to see don Hilde with this malady—approximately 10 percent of his clientele—had few physical symptoms or physical complaints. Ayahuasca played a role in diagnosing the syndrome.

The folklore of salt gives us some insight into this illness, and why salt is vital and yet feared. When salt is placed on a living plant, it destroys it. This contrasts with the vital role that salt has in maintaining health, especially in hot climates. Since ancient times, central Amazon Indians obtained salt by trade or made long and perilous journeys to the salt mountain in Chanchamayo to gather salt until they were forcibly stopped by European colonists in Peru in the nineteenth century. It is interesting to note that the salt taboo still exists for people who drink ayahuasca tea in an attempt to obtain a vision that will enable them to fix the source of witchcraft. In fact, throughout the world, salt taboos tend to be found among traditional users of plant hallucinogens.

Salt plays an important role in preserving meats and fish, and salted foods were traditionally an important part of preservation techniques among farmers and city dwellers who couldn't afford electricity and refrigeration. Even the Spanish word for salary, *salario*, derives from the Latin *salarium*, for the money given to Roman soldiers to buy salt—which attests to the important role this substance has had historically in trade and barter worldwide.

The link between salt and bad luck can probably be traced to periods of commerce during the colonial period, when the chemical action of salt on containers caused their decay and corroded steel on transport boats. Salt became incorporated into the nefarious ingredients in popular witchcraft hexes, mixed with earth from cemeteries or inorganic remains, then used to bewitch people. Even today, when an unwelcome visitor is in one's house, Amazonian people believe that throwing salt on the fire will hasten that person's departure.

During my February 1979 study of don Hilde, when my family and I lived in his home, I was able to describe this misfortune syndrome. Saladera is linked to an evildoer who places salt on the threshold of a person's home or slips noxious ingredients into a drink to cause subsequent bad luck in love, work, and friendship. Unlike other illnesses that cause physical suffering, patients who came to see don Hilde complained only that they had been bewitched and now suffer from misfortune or bad luck. In their words, they were "salted," and everything in their life has soured—their work, their home, a love affair, or their relationships with their children, spouse, or in-laws. In fact, whatever can possibly go wrong does.

In this part of the world, the consistent experience of bad luck or generalized misfortune is not perceived as occurring by mere chance. To the contrary, people are quick to project their feelings that they are the victims of bad luck outward toward significant others in their lives whose malice, envy, or anger they believe is directed against themselves. Malevolent neighbors or work colleagues are identified as the source of and therefore responsible for this bewitchment. The constant aggravation or persistent difficulties encountered in finding a job are not necessarily attributed to a person's own individual inadequacy. Rarely is such failure abstracted, for instance to economic causes, but rather is widely attributed to others' spitefulness.

The ten adult patients of don Hilde who complained of saladera during the time I spent there were different than the others he saw that month of February. All were highly anxious. The women— women appear to be the more frequent victims of saladera—cried a lot and several said they couldn't work, had poor concentration, and were fearful of the future. They all told don Hilde that they had saladera and had generally made self-diagnoses before they sought his help. Unlike other witchcraft illnesses in the Amazon, saladera doesn't require that a witch be consulted for that person to make bad luck appear. Rather, a man or woman can directly cause this to occur in another by insinuating a potion into that person's drink or by throwing a foul substance across their threshold.

Don Hilde's patients told me specifically how saladera could be caused. Menstrual blood would be collected, along with other noxious substances, which were secretly introduced as a potion into a drink called a *pusanga* by women of dubious morality who wished to break up a marriage and lure a man away from his wife and family. (The recurrent theme about the power of menstrual blood is found throughout the Amazon and in prehistoric tribal life; its taboo is widespread. Even at the time of this study, women's activities on a day-to-day basis are restrained when they menstruate, especially the prohibition on entering the forests to gather plants, on weeding gardens, or on traveling on the rivers.) Vultures' feces mixed with water and menstrual blood, dropped at someone's doorstep, is a sure way to make misfortune happen to another. Salt, when thrown across a neighbor's threshold or placed on a windowsill, is enough provocation for a person to change her residence, since it is believed that catastrophe or death will follow.

The women who complained of suffering from saladera were very often single mothers, abandoned by their spouses or common-law partners. They went to healers like don Hilde to ask for his help with the ayahuasca potion to make their spouse return to them. Don Hilde saw about fifty new cases of saladera a year. Once don Hilde diagnosed the illness, he would prescribe a series of herbal baths for them, taken in the evening in his home. After drying off, the patient was instructed to remain in her clothing for a twenty-four-hour period. Most clients did not believe that saladera would respond to medical attention in the city.

Actually, don Hilde treated Yando and me preventively for saladera as we were getting ready to leave Pucallpa. Each of us took a bath with fragrant antiwitchcraft herbs. When we were dry, we had to remain in the same clothing for a full twenty-four hours so that the measures would take effect. And it seemed to me that things did go well for us afterward.

PARANOIA AND *BANISTERIOPSIS* IN WITCHCRAFT AND HEALING IN IQUITOS, PERU

I spent the first twelve years of my life growing up in the Bronx, New York, where there were no boas around, except perhaps at the Bronx Zoo! There was no witchcraft either! Much to my surprise, I had hardly arrived in the Amazon before lurid tales of bewitchment and tales of vicious harm to my informants were related to me.

As a psychology major in college I had read a lot about psychopathology, and I began to see a link between witchcraft beliefs and what psychiatrists call paranoia. Ayahuasca healers assembled men and women from among the urban poor and held ritual sessions to drink ayahuasca two to three times a week, generally in jungle clearings at the edge of the city. Both patients and healers would drink an infusion made from boiling the vine several hours, mixed with chacruna (*Psychotria viridis*). Tobacco was often smoked during the session by the healer.

One of the main functions of the ayahuasca healer's ritual was to exorcise evil spirits that were believed to have entered the sick person's body, lanced through the air by an evil witch. The healer blew tobacco smoke over the patient's body or sucked at painful parts of it. Little did we know then that the neurochemistry and imaging technology that emerged in the millennium (as demonstrated in 2006 in the work of the researcher Dr. Jean Gehrighe of the University of California, Irvine) would document the anxiety-diminishing properties of secondary smoke. All I knew then was that I would come home from these sessions smelling like a busy barmaid! In the sessions, *icaros,* special ayahuasca songs, were sung, and there were whistling incantations throughout the several hours that the ritual lasted. I was able to describe particular cultural syndromes of illness, including the one called *daño,* which attributed the cause of evildoing either to neighbors or disgruntled relatives, resulting in physical illness.

The concepts we have in Western society about good and evil don't really convey Amazonian worldviews particularly well. Although most ayahuasca healers were called on to heal patients who believed they had been bewitched, there is an element of moral arbitration on the part of the healer, who often claims to use countermagic to return the evil to its perpetrator. In this way he will relieve and even cure his patient's symptoms. Some healers report that they use the purge, as ayahuasca is called, only for socially valued ends—to cure illness. But they often speak of cases of people who came to them to ask them to inflict harm on another toward whom they might bear a grudge, be envious of, or angry at. Most of the healers I worked with denied they ever used ayahuasca for evil purposes, but brujos could be easily identified in all Amazon cities and rural areas. These witches specialized in using the purge purely for nefarious ends, and they collected a hefty fee in advance. They used both psychic means (evil-willing) and plants that kill to harm the intended victim. These toxic plants can be slipped secretly into a beverage at a party or made to fall on the skin of a victim when that person passed a secluded spot. Sometimes the witch boasted that he controlled certain spirits that he could summon to inflict harm on a designated victim.

Some societies appear to institutionalize and regularly produce in their members disordered behavior patterns. The anthropologist John G. Kennedy pointed out several general characteristics that link witchcraft beliefs and paranoid delusions, which certainly describe the belief systems I observed in Iquitos and Salas. The content of the beliefs is what we in Euroamerican society consider impossible; mystical causation just is not part of Western cognitions, and evidence-based cause-and-effect relationships are the norm. Then there is the unshakable conviction and certainty of those who believe in witchcraft, in which any disconfirming experiences are ignored or brushed away. Such people harbor great suspiciousness and fear of external threats. The delusions have kernels of truth to them, and indeed there may be the actual existence of hostility in interpersonal relationships. A pseudocommunity of real and imagined persons is said to be present (in this case, animal familiars), and the delusions are part of a closed logical system that explains and interprets events. From a psychoanalytic perspective, this system is a projection to defend the individual against anxiety.

Certainly when we look at Belen in those early years of my studies, interpersonal relations among the urban poor were laden with anxiety and filled with great tension and strife. I was interested to see that one mestizo healer I interviewed in September 2007 talked about clients asking him to bewitch or kill an enemy, which he refused to do. This was almost forty years after I had left Belen, but despite major culture change and modernization, some things change very slowly or not at all.

Economic problems confronted slum residents as farming lands became scarce and natural resources such as fish and game fast disappeared with indiscriminate use. The daily life of the destitute, who live in some twenty different slum settlements throughout Iquitos when I conducted my study in the late 1960s, showed a high incidence of social pathology, including family disorganization, abandonment of children, and prostitution. The belief that ill will existed on the part of others was widespread, and neither relatives nor neighbors were exempt from the pervasive belief that at bottom, people were envious and jealous of others and wished them harm.

There are some interesting parallels in the Amazon to these paranoid delusional systems. The impossible content or mystical causation, such as people reporting that they have flown through the air and experienced ephemeral spiritual beings, some of whom they say they can control for ulterior purposes, seems bizarre to Westerners. Some ayahuasqueros say they can leave their bodies and enter those of their enemies to inflict incurable diseases on them. Some thirty-six different poisonous plants in the northwest Amazon have been documented, which indicates the extent of possibilities for poisoning.

Another delusion, the imperviousness to disconfirming experience, is noted in the occurrence of suspiciousness and fear of external threat. Once, an alleged witch overreacted in the presence of a colleague of mine, a psychiatrist, at an ayahuasca session. The reputed witch had not been told that my colleague was a medical doctor. The man came to see me the next day to accuse me of having tried to trick him. I admit that he watched my house carefully afterward, and I actually feared that his suspicion that I would initiate police action against him would lead to my suffering dire consequences, such as being poisoned. Fortunately, he went on a long trip and my fears diminished.

The belief in witchcraft is a closed logical system and has sustaining mechanisms. In Peru, when sick people go to paramedics in the city for medical help, they often worsen. The patient cites this as proof that he is bewitched, not that the paramedic is poorly trained or may use medicines whose potency has expired. At this point a countermagician will be sought to return the evil to its source. The ayahuasca visions are interpreted by the healer to identify the originator of the evil. The healer's role is to reestablish equilibrium in the realm of health.

In terms of the mechanisms of projection to defend oneself against anxiety, beliefs in witches and evil-willing are culturally constituted defense mechanisms that enable people to deal with problems of survival and stability in their lives. An argument for the application of theories of paranoia to life in the northwest Amazon could be easily made.

WHAT WE CAN
LEARN FROM SHAMANIC HEALING

As a psychotherapist in practice since the mid-1980s who has worked extensively with Latino immigrants in Southern California, I realized right from the beginning of my psychotherapy work that there was a good deal that I had learned from the shamanic healing I had studied in Peru that could be applied in the treatment of my clients in Southern California. Such an approach is particularly useful among the urban poor and rural immigrants in the United States whose numbers are increasing every year.

At the time of this writing, for example, one in ten California residents is foreign-born and many are Latino. I was able to draw from a database of more than 700 Latino immigrant families that I treated over the years to demonstrate concepts and techniques of psychotherapeutic intervention derived from shamanic roots in the immigrants' original culture. Clearly, I was not personally involved with hallucinogenic plants in this endeavor, but I did draw from the shamanic concept of making an altered state of consciousness available to clients.

With that in mind, I learned hypnosis and relaxation therapies and provided clients with a free hypnosis cassette tape and eventually a CD for home use, to alleviate symptoms of anxiety and insomnia. A second technique I picked up from shamanic healers was that of behavior modification, in which shamans use principles of learning theory to rearrange their clients' lives and alleviate stressors in their environment. A third technique was that of cognitive restructuring—teaching clients to be as rational as possible in addressing their multiple problems.

As I have already noted, in Peru the shaman spontaneously enters into an altered state of consciousness, controlling the trance and entering it readily, at will. This state is used to predict the future, to metaphorically experience a change in his shape, and to contact spiritual entities to use to conquer evil, negate hexes, neutralize witchcraft, and restore the client to good health. Hypnosis, the Western answer to creating a state of suggestibility amid an altered state of consciousness, is a very powerful tool that can be used with Latino immigrants in either English or Spanish to create an altered state. This light trance alleviates symptoms and can tone the client's parasympathetic nervous system. The therapist enables the client to enter into an altered state of consciousness conducive to healing and provides the client with personal control over her own body chemistry. In this special state, the therapist's suggestions are more readily followed and therapeutic goals can be enhanced.

Healers I studied in Peru are quick to demonstrate their power and control over the healing milieu. In Salas, one healer came to the outdoor healing area wearing a fine alpaca poncho that everyone admired. He boasted about how he was given this fine garment because of his success in curing a client. Shortly afterward, back in the United States, I visited a well-known psychiatrist in New York to discuss my research findings. He was an established author and administrator in that state's mental-health community. The doctor had a fine townhouse on Park Avenue with a Japanese garden at the entrance and original Picasso prints adorning the walls. It was hard to see any difference between the fine poncho in rural Peru and the trappings of wealth and success in the New York townhouse. Of course, each example made sense within its own cultural matrix.

AYAHUASCA AND TOBACCO SMOKE: HEALING OR HARMFUL?

When I took ayahuasca in Iquitos in 1968, I found that the plant produced what psychiatrists call an anxiolytic effect—that is, it diminishes feelings of anxiety and effects an afterglow. As I mentioned, before I took ayahuasca, at the beginning of my fieldwork, I was feeling alone, with little emotional support. While I wasn't deeply depressed, I did cross the days off a calendar as if I were in jail. Ayahuasca is a difficult treatment for mild depression, and, of course, the cost is high for the person taking it: vomiting, diarrhea, nausea, and the like. Whereas in my childhood in the Bronx, a parent might take a vomiting child to the emergency room of the nearby city hospital, in the Amazon, where airborne spores of worms (resulting in helminthic disease) are commonplace, mothers purge their children periodically. The ayahuasca experience to alleviate anxiety, too, is quite different from the pharmaceutical pills available in the United States, Europe, and elsewhere to treat this syndrome.

Historically, ayahuasca has been and continues to be used widely in the Amazon to provide revelations or truths about deeply held beliefs concerning witchcraft and evil. Thus the person who becomes ill, often with a sudden pain or discomfort, would seek out an ayahuasca healer, drink the tea, and see a panorama of events generally involving an envious relative or neighbor, a spurned lover, or just an obnoxious and vindictive person who might pay a witch to harm him. Furthermore, since the healer would drink the ayahuasca with his client, he, too, would see the origin of the witchcraft-derived illness, and with his shamanic power, be able to redirect the evil back to the perpetrator. Only then would he prescribe herbs and treatments for the client.

The concept that the plant itself was the cure for the illness does not exist. Instead, the revelations that come with taking ayahuasca are said to uncover truth—the truth believed by both healer and patient to be at the root of the problem. Moreover, as with don Hilde, the plant confers information to the healer about which herbs to mix together to prepare for his patient, so that the patient's symptoms will also be alleviated. From a psychiatric point of view, the faith of the patient in the healer is paramount. His suggestions can only lead to a diminishing of symptoms. It's like when you leave your doctor's office with a prescription in hand, and you haven't even filled the prescription yet you have a feeling of relief knowing that you've been helped and will get better.

Among the strongest memories I have of the Amazon are the many times I attended ayahuasca healing sessions and had tobacco smoke blown over my back, my neck, and the top of my head by the healer, as I sat and observed the sessions. The tobacco used is called *mapacho,* the vernacular name for rolled *Nicotiana rustica.* Its use is a long-honored tradition in the Amazon. The smoke is secondary in nature, and during the year of field-work (1968–69), I never, ever smoked even one cigarette. Nonetheless, I had always had an interest in tobacco since psychiatrist Oscar Janiger and I published two papers in the 1970s on the suggestive hallucinogenic properties of tobacco, a theme dear to Dr. Janiger's heart.

My part of the research was to review data from the Human Relations Area Files, a database of ethnographic materials on nearly 400 groups worldwide, compiled by anthropologists over the years. Certainly we know that traditional cultures, particularly those in the West, use tobacco and its derivatives as facilitating agents in religious and ceremonial trance induction, witchcraft, divination, and healing ceremonies.

Two chemicals from the harmala alkaloids—harman and norharman—have been isolated from cured commercial tobaccos and their smoke. They constitute a chemical group, the beta-carbolines, in which several closely related members with similar pharmacological properties have been found to be hallucinogenic. These substances cross the blood-brain barrier and change the neural transmission in the visual system. The tobacco that the Native Americans smoked was quite different from Virginia tobacco. Commercial tobacco is produced in other southern states as well, particularly the Carolinas. The tobacco used in Native American culture created a strong narcotic state and knocked the Indians out, allowing the user to have visions that would have been significant to the culture.

In the original research that Dr. Janiger and I published, we looked at such topics as magical-religious use of tobacco in the West, tobacco for divination, tobacco to treat disease, and tobacco for hedonistic goals. Tobacco smoke among many rainforest Amazonian tribes was used to induce trance, dreams, and visions and was an important adjunct to sha-

manistic techniques. Certainly it was an accompaniment to the ingestion of ayahuasca in curing rituals.

In 1987 the anthropologist Johannes Wilbert documented the role
of tobacco in South American shamanism. Tobacco smoke occupied an
important place in rituals, and blowing smoke over the body of a patient
was a common way of expelling pathogenic spirits and purifying. Patients
were literally fumigated with clouds of smoke, as this was believed to
protect those clients from harm, despite any long-term effects on health.
Among some tribal groups, smoke is blown not only over practitioners
but also over their paraphernalia of curing as well, prior to drinking ayahuasca. The smoke is seen as a preventive measure to effect a cure or
bring good fortune. Tobacco is an important resource, as 72 percent of
the plant species are found in the Americas and include both *Nicotiana
rustica* and *Nicotiana tabacum.* Wilbert found that there were more than
133 tribal groups that used tobacco in this manner.

Can you imagine my surprise, then, when at an academic function
at the University of California, Irvine, in late 2007, I chatted with a
colleague of mine in the psychiatry department, only to learn that several researchers working on tobacco use among youth had found out
that persons with emotional dysfunctions are most at risk to initiate
smoking and to become addicted to nicotine? Using neuroscience brain
imaging, these researchers found that smoking regulates attention and
emotions. People with strong dysfunctions tend to smoke at high rates
and have less success in stopping smoking.

Research by Dr. Jean Gehricke and colleagues found that adolescents in the United States may self-medicate with tobacco to regulate
negative emotions associated with their problems of attention and
depression. Nicotine treatment diminishes peoples' dysfunction when
they are depressed. In particular, what the psychiatrists call internalizing behavior is used for problems such as major depression, anxiety
disorders, and negative emotions. More evidence is accumulating on the
brain mechanisms for this effect.

Certainly we can argue that native Amazonian shamans were quite aware of the medicinal benefits of ayahuasca and tobacco smoke and incorporated both of these into their pharmacopoeia of healing plants. As imaging techniques yield more information so that we can understand the health potential of these plants, we can expect that ancient wisdom will carry the day!

KETAMINE USE IN A BURN CENTER: HALLUCINOGEN OR DEBRIDEMENT FACILITATOR?

In the 1980s, when my work at the UC Irvine Regional Burn Center was in full force, I realized that the major pharmaceutical agent being used in debridement—the surgical removal of dead skin from burn patients—was the hallucinogen ketamine. An unusual anesthesia since its introduction in 1962, it has varied medical uses despite its reported LSD-like effects on patients. The psychedelic is used because of its short action and the fact that it doesn't negatively affect breathing. Moreover, the patient is able to move his body as the debridement takes place.

Nevertheless, studies show that 12 to 36 percent of the patients anesthetized with this drug suffer distressing emergent reactions such that even when low doses are used, these postoperative reactions are not eliminated. Side effects of ketamine on burn patients include agitation, vivid dreams, bizarre and impulsive behavior, dissociation, paranoia, and hallucinations. After the drug wears off, patients report flashbacks. The patient's psychological status prior to taking ketamine anesthesia can affect his reaction to the hallucinogenic properties of the drug. What I realized when speaking to the head nurse was that her technique of preparing patients to undergo ketamine anesthesia, which she came upon in a logical manner, was very much akin to the tribal use of hallucinogens I had observed. I helped to write up the ongoing study in 1985 for publication in the *Journal of Psychoactive Drugs.*

Unlike other such drugs, ketamine selectively blocks pain conduction and perception and leaves those parts of the central nervous system not participating in pain transmission and perception free from the depressant effects of the drug. The patient appears not to be asleep, but dissociated from his surroundings. Many patients experienced vivid, colorful dreams when administered ketamine, or the feeling of floating or flying in outer space. My cross-cultural research has shown that we cannot predict the drug effect without taking into consideration what precedes it, that is, the "antecedent variables" mentioned earlier.

In a burn center like that at UC Irvine, we found that our goal was to institute measures to make the experience less frightening or psychologically damaging. Patients at the center have only recently endured the negative experience of being burned. Such emotional factors as fear, despair, and uncertainty are at play among these people; their emotional state is compounded by constant pain, accentuated in every aspect of the patient's surroundings, from bed linen to air flow. In preparation for their ketamine anesthesia, they were mostly instructed by doctors and nurses that the experience would be pleasant for them. The head nurse, Suzanne Martinez, who was preparing her M.A. thesis based on this research, queried the patients and they completed a questionnaire regarding their ketamine experiences. The nurses and physicians would prepare the patients for the ketamine experience by means of an unstructured, informal discussion of the procedure, mentioning the likelihood that positive thoughts would result in a pleasant experience for them. A higher percentage of the patients who were prepared in this way by physicians, as compared to nurses, told the investigators that their subsequent experience was not frightening. Twelve of the fifteen subjects stated that they experienced dreams while under the influence of ketamine, and eight described them as pleasant. Forty percent chose descriptions of their dreams as frightening, 73 percent chose the term *floating* to describe their dreams, and only two subjects described the experience as beautiful. Seventy-three percent said the event was confusing.

Just as with tribal societies in which hallucinogens are used in religion or rites of passage, the expectations of the person being administered the hallucinogen will influence the outcome. People perceived as having status will be paid more attention to than those seen as being lower in the hierarchy. This is true whether the setting is a tropical jungle or a highly sanitized intensive-care unit of a teaching hospital.

11

Psychedelics, Art, Music, and Creativity

ONE CANNOT PRESUME TO WRITE about psychedelics and culture without some focus on music, art, and theater, as these are part of the psychedelic aesthetic experience of the person who uses ayahuasca, mescaline, or other psychedelic substances. This section summarizes not only the role of music—whistling, singing, and percussion—in the ayahuasca experience but also looks at how music actually programs the psychedelic visual and spiritual experience. Moreover, the theatrical aspects of the experience, staged by the shaman, must be analyzed as well.

I also look at LSD and art in the context of Oscar Janiger's study, which included a sample of 100 artists who experienced the effects of psychedelics on their creative abilities. Additionally, in 2005, an exhibit was mounted in Los Angeles by the Museum of Contemporary Art called Ecstasy: In and About Altered States. Finally, I examine the changing canons of taste and values for these substances in contemporary urban society.

HALLUCINOGENIC RITUAL AS THEATER

Throughout the world, at all levels of social complexity, the expressive elements of the hallucinogenic drug experience have been reported. In 1979 I examined the expressive and theatrical dimension of cross-cultural hallucinogenic ritual. For the anthropologist studying the use of psychedelics, who watches other people imbibe hallucinogenic teas like ayahuasca, one can only comment on the lack of theatricality in coastal and Amazonian healing rituals.

After a while it became boring for me, as I sat around a circle and watched others with their eyes closed as the shaman whistled or chanted quietly. Occasionally someone would get up to vomit away from the group or relieve himself. It seems that the internalized thespian flavor of the hallucinogenic ritual is not amenable to superficial observation by an outsider looking in. Yet the teas contain within them the intrinsic power to provoke expressive experiences equal in force and drama to the best theater available in any city, in any part of the civilized world.

The urban theater buff finds her way to a physical structure called a theater. Inside this center are found actors who render a script about life that another person has imaginatively created to imitate actual life, so that an audience registers its emotional impact. At times, this may even result in a catharsis of emotions in the best of the Aristotelian tradition.

The hallucinogenic journey is another genre of drama completely. In the healing ritual, the person who imbibes is actor, playwright, stage director, costumer, and makeup artist—and even musician. The fast-moving, brilliant kaleidoscope of colors, forms, geometric patterns, movement, and counterpoint are easily among the most unique experiences that most people ever have in normal waking consciousness. Moreover, this is produced entirely from within the person's own psyche. There is staging involved in the presence of shamanic guidance of the hallucinogenic journey. One of the most important functions of the psychedelic guide is to produce music through chants, whistling, and percussion, which evokes patterned visions that have specific cultural meaning within the context of the experience. In the Amazon, the music helps the patient see the boa, the mother spirit of the plant.

Shamans guiding their clients' hallucinogenic experiences recognize synesthesia, a jumble of sensory input, in their clients. The shaman guides these interior dramas, which take place in natural settings, and uses odors, sounds, visual cues, and tactile aids to enhance the hallucinogenic effects, which contribute to the overall drama.

Visions are generally culturally patterned in traditional hallucinogenic-using societies of the world. Each group member who imbibes will have visions that are shared by his fellows, evoked by a shamanic guide whose role is to create music to summon these culture-specific visions. The stereotypic visionary experience thus functions as a hallucinogenic "script" that is derived both by the individual and the group.

HALLUCINOGENIC MUSIC: THE JUNGLE GYM IN CONSCIOUSNESS

A colleague of mine at Cal State Fullerton, Fred Katz, is a well-known jazz musician and was interested in the music I had taped in Belen. The music fell into two categories: secular varieties and ayahuasca ritual whistling and chants. In the 1970s very little had been written about the function of music in psychedelic sessions outside of the United States. Katz and I decided to analyze the music I had taped. At first I was certain that the music was simply background music, to relax and calm the person—in the realm of special effects, tangential to the healing experience. As we listened to the tapes and put the music into perspective, however, our evaluation changed. We realized that the whistling incantations during psychedelic intoxication served as a vital link to bridge separate realities induced by the ingestion of plant hallucinogens.

From here it was a logical next step to examine the music in other societies in which normal waking consciousness is altered by plant hallucinogenic ritual, to see what patterns emerged. The research question we asked was: why is music is so integral a part of psychedelic ceremonies in traditional Native American societies? We realized that indeed music was not tangential to the psychedelic experience, whether the ritual was for purposes of healing, achieving contact with the supernatural, divining the future, or for recreation or pleasure.

Ayahuasca music is used only in ritual ceremonies. It is tempting to suggest a comparison between ayahuasca whistling incantations and music such as Gregorian chanting, insofar as the basic function of the two goes. One could argue that Gregorian chants and ecclesiastic modes represent tonal relationships in which scales are structured so as to evoke a spiritual experience within the context of Christianity. Perhaps the ayahuasca music can be viewed as an essential component of a nonordinary reality sustained by the sensory overload inherent in the hallucinogenic-induced alteration of consciousness.

This music cannot be divorced from its social context. The perception of time slowing down or changing while a person is under the influence of ayahuasca has to be related to how the music is perceived by the person under the influence of the harmine and harmaline present in the ayahuasca potion. Visions change frequently from fast to slow and are controlled and evoked by the healer, who is the creative force in deciding which melodies to call upon. Healers claim that the choice of the melodies they create can alleviate the patient's nausea and cause it to pass.

Healers make it very clear that it is their decision as to which melodies to play, to evoke certain types of visions. Slower incantations may be responsible for oft-reported visions of men and women who are later identified as evildoers. Most ayahuasca sessions show that about 75 percent of those ingesting the plant tea do experience heavy vomiting or nausea. Since the hallucinogen causes dissolution of ego boundaries, and also has the potential to generate extreme anxiety, music, with its own implicit structure, provides a set of banisters and pathways through which the person imbibing is able to negotiate his way. This is generally done so that the person can achieve his culture's goal of psychedelic use—namely, to obtain a stereotypic visionary experience that has been programmed by the society.

In that article, we decided to assemble data on hallucinogenic rituals and music, focusing on traditional societies of the Americas. We looked at the type of music, the ritual and its function, the plants used, ritual activities, and who was performing. My earlier work was a useful jumping-off point for testing the hypothesis that to predict the effects of psychotropic substances we have to pay attention to cultural variables such as values, beliefs, and expectations in the society where plant hallucinogens are used.

Sudden access to the unconscious is not part and parcel of normal waking activity. People may differ in their ability to handle these relatively unknown realms of the psyche when they are made accessible by the ingestion of a plant psychedelic. Under these circumstances, anxiety may be expressed in a number of ways: vomiting, diarrhea, nausea, cramps, extreme tachycardia, rise of blood pressure—all components of the so-called bad trip reported in all cultures for which there is adequate data. It is almost as if once the lid of the Pandora's box of psychedelic experiences is raised, anything can emerge. In his 1972 study of LSD ingestion in Western culture, Stanislav Grof, in an attempt to explain the near universality of these kinds of effects, described the frequent occurrence of things like the appearance of monsters and horrendous creatures of the psyche and revisited birth trauma and fetal expulsion from the womb. Interestingly enough, none of my Amazonian clients ever reported such experiences in their ayahuasca sessions.

When Katz and I evaluated all the music data, we could only marvel at the pervasive presence of music in a variety of forms, as an integral part of the psychedelic experience. The participant in the ritual perceives the implicit structure of music quite differently from during his normal waking consciousness.

We know of course of the mathematical precision and structure found in all music. Once the biochemical effects of a hallucinogen alter the user's perception, music operates like a jungle gym in consciousness. We use the concept of the jungle gym in a metaphoric sense, to visualize the familiar children's playground architecture, comprised of iron bars interlinked in horizontal and vertical planes. In contrast to the playtime structure where the child chooses spontaneous pathways and heights to explore, the admixture of music in the ayahuasca experience functions almost like a blueprint. The implicit mathematical structure of music, purposefully chosen or created by the shaman, serves specific cultural goals—to see the boa guardian spirit of the ayahuasca vine and to achieve contact with special supernatural deities. The jungle gym is an inflexible system in which the choice of pathway is left to the child. Similarly, music, also a fixed structure, is imposed on the imbiber by the shaman, who controls to some degree his clients' visual options within this ritualized use of music.

Shamans state that the music they create provokes special types of visions. Healers told me that the particular traditional melodies, icaros, that they chose to sing or whistle would evoke visions they specifically desired their clients to have, to permit them to see the agent responsible for bewitchment, to resolve anxiety created in the wake of psychedelic use, and so on.

Moreover, a recurrent theme in tribal and Third World societies where psychedelics are used is the cultural patterning of hallucinogenic experience. This stereotyping of visionary content gives us a glimpse into how a person's psyche is subject to cultural conditioning. These stereotypic visions are eagerly sought after, generally as a sign that contact with the realm of the sacred is occurring and that some message, omen, or knowledge will be passed on to the initiate. Hallucinogenic plants are used in this way to reaffirm the values of a society and to make available supernatural forces, both visually and emotionally.

In evaluating the music, one general characteristic, or the lowest common denominator, appears to be the frequency of rattling sounds, almost always along with whistling or singing or rapid vibratory sounds. Rattles, singing, chanting, and vocalizing in general are an important part of the hallucinogenic experience, in that the jungle gym is built up, torn down, or rearranged in a sort of child's game of consciousness block-building to serve specific cultural goals. The implicit structure of music fills the void left by the effects of the psychedelic and offers a new structure to the participant, which shamans use in the service of culturally valued goals.

LSD, SPIRITUALITY, AND THE CREATIVE PROCESS

In 1954 psychiatrist Oscar Janiger began experimenting with a then new chemical discovery known as LSD–25. Over an eight-year period, Janiger gave LSD to more than 950 men and women, ranging in age from eighteen to eighty-one, and coming from all walks of life. A large amount of data was collected, including follow-up studies done forty years later.

I met Dr. Janiger when I returned to California in 1969, and we became friends over the years. He always spoke of his research, but aside from some interviews in the alternative press the materials were never published. Janiger and I published two articles on tobacco's possible hallucinogenic link, as well as a summary of his early research with LSD and creativity. Shortly before he passed away in 2002, we decided to prepare a book that would make this historic material available to the public. Of great interest was a subset of 100 artists and writers in Los Angeles who were given LSD. The acid was pure and was provided by Sandoz Pharmaceutical Company. All participants were given the substance in a controlled and safe environment, a private home rented for the experiment. Janiger's general aim was to explore and study the effects of LSD on a large, highly differentiated group of people in a natural setting. Simply speaking, Janiger wanted to discover what LSD did to the average person. Was there such a thing as an intrinsic characteristic LSD response? During the course of his work, he identified twenty-eight common responses that he considered core characteristics of the LSD experience.

Janiger's research took place at a moment in history that can never be repeated, a time uncontaminated by either expectation or hype, when

Dr. Janiger's Kachina doll rendered
by an artist when in a normal
state of consciousness.

there was little knowledge or understanding of the effects of this powerful substance and its influence in deconditioning a person from strongly held beliefs, values, and ways of thinking and feeling.

In the book *LSD, Spirituality, and the Creative Process,* which was published in 2003, a year after Janiger's death, I was able to delineate the characteristics of the LSD experience and look at the artwork produced by the small group of professional artists who were very enthusiastic about its effects. Some 24 percent of the participants, without any prompting from Janiger, had a spiritual experience that was very meaningful to them, even in an environment that was banal and ordinary. My job was to add a cultural dimension to the study. Janiger's data sought to reveal the idiosyncratic effects of LSD on his volunteers; the data did indeed reveal a marked pattern of idiosyncrasy in which volunteers viewed the psychophysiological effects of LSD through private lenses of their own life histories. It soon became clear that there was no boa in Los Angeles either!

When we looked at the data I had accumulated on ayahuasca and other plant hallucinogens over the years and contrasted it to Janiger's findings, we saw some telling similarities. Animism of nature and objects is found in both samples. Vibratory energy is reported in tribal

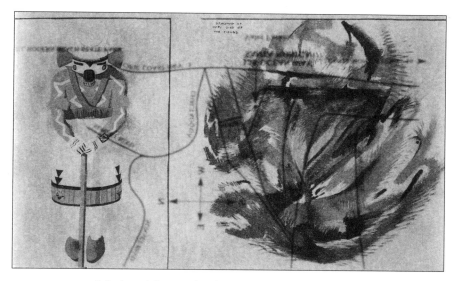

A Kachina doll painted under normal conditions (left), and
one hour later after LSD had been ingested (right).

and urban groups. At high dosages, the hidden or critical observer was
obliterated, and pure sensory data reigned. There was some degree of
group cohesion and bonding. When people were prepared for or had
an individual proclivity toward spiritual life, the LSD-like experience
could provide entry into another dimension, a special place or sanctu-
ary with significant meaning. In all cases, the powerful chemicals created a highly suggestible state in those who imbibed—so powerful that
some of Janiger's volunteers reported an almost hypnotic compulsion to
execute suggestions, even when none were given.

ECSTASY: IN AND ABOUT ALTERED STATES

After the start of the millennium, there seemed to be a change in general
societal attitudes about psychedelics. For one thing, more research on
the medical potentials of the plants has been taking place, and a number
of studies have been spearheaded by the Multidisciplinary Association
of Psychedelic Studies (MAPS), a nonprofit group that funds research.

Also active in this research has been the Heffter Research Institute in New Mexico. The arts have not been left behind in the wave of interest and expression of values connected to psychedelics.

On October 5, 2005, the Museum of Contemporary Art in Los Angeles mounted an exhibit called Ecstasy: In and About Altered States. I reviewed the catalog for a psychiatry journal, with no pretensions regarding the pathology of hallucinogen use, nor the beauty, aesthetics, and meanings of experiences. The exhibit, which ran until February 20, 2006, included the art of thirty internationally known artists. The work displayed addressed both agents and effects of altered consciousness.

The psychiatric definition of ecstasy is that of a trance state in which religious ideas or other similar ideas of dedication and complete surrender occupy almost the entire field of consciousness. Of course ecstasy is also the street name for the drug MDMA and brings to mind the psychedelic agents and the phenylethylamines used in American and European club culture to facilitate huge raves. In these events, thousands of revelers come together to dance until dawn in abandoned warehouses to the beat of acid and techno music.

I lived through the 1960s as a young, aspiring medical anthropologist and spent time in San Francisco as well as Los Angeles. It was clear to me that the art of this exhibit was quite different from what I had observed in the 1960s. Ensconced in separate units of the museum, which covered thousands of square feet, the work of the exhibition's artists displayed images of ecstatic states. The artists and their statements in the catalog were driven by utopian faith in the capacity of art to expand and alter perception and consciousness. The chief curator, Peter Schimmel, argued that the experience of art is, in itself, an altered state. Various comments in the catalog spoke of how youth attains physical release through dancing and consumption of substances such as ecstasy, marijuana, mushrooms, and LSD.

The drug ecstasy has become emblematic of a social movement that has attracted increasing numbers of disaffected youth in Europe and North America. Ecstasy is said to provide intense feelings of connectedness with one's companions and humanity in general, reminding us of some of the anthropological writings of the 1960s and 1970s. In particular, one recalls the anthropologist Janet Siskind's documentation in 1973 of how ayahuasca taken by in-marrying brothers-in-law among one rainforest group enabled those who had previously been strangers to one another to be able to be of one heart, to work together, and to share resources.

Other societies that I have discussed in this book have incorporated psychedelics into adolescent initiation ceremonies to create such feelings of connectedness. This contrasts with contemporary urban society in which ecstasy is just one more scheduled drug with legal repercussions for youthful offenders. Without control or vigilance, their use of the substance is merely a form of escapism and irrational hedonism. Nonetheless, early anecdotal reports of ecstasy touted its use in effectively facilitating psychotherapy.

The art displayed at the museum was different from that of tribal societies. Lacking religious values, meaning, and the sacred in connection with the chemical, this art was clever and challenging but self-contained. It didn't flow from one space to another like the psychedelic experience does. Aside from some pieces of spectacular color, the exhibit was muted, with lots of gimmicks such as a space with red and white *Amanita muscaria* (fly agaric) mushrooms in polymer plastic suspended from the ceiling.

The catalog linked contemporary interest in ecstatic states to the ancient Greeks and beyond. Eighteenth-century romanticism was featured, as well as surrealism with Dali, Miro, Picasso, and Tanguay, who explored the realm of the unconscious and dream states. The catalog certainly functioned as a counterpoint to the negative valence that the altered state has in Western society and may mirror a change in attitude about the acceptance of these substances. Only time will tell.

12

Psychedelics and the
União do Vegetal Church

AS A CONSEQUENCE OF TWO trips I made to Brazil in the late 1990s, I collaborated with a binational research team to study a fast-growing new religious group with temples throughout Brazil and the United States. The cities we visited were Rio de Janeiro, São Paulo, Brasilia, and Manaus. Research summarized in this section examines the União do Vegetal Church (UDV) and its structure, a religious institution in which ayahuasca is a sacrament. Our particular focus was on adolescent members, who were permitted by the church to take ayahuasca twice each month. In addition, we looked at the concept of drug substitution as redemption, which was documented by fieldwork inquiries with eleven *mestres,* or church elders.

AYAHUASCA USE FROM A
CROSS-CULTURAL PERSPECTIVE

The União do Vegetal Church was founded in Brazil in 1962 and has a current membership of more than 9,000 people in more than 100 *nucleos,* or communities, both in Brazil and abroad. Ayahuasca is associated with different religions in Brazil, including the UDV, Santo Daime, and Barquinha. The plant has been traditionally used in the context of Indian societies and also among the nonindigenous populations, generally in locations remote from urban areas. The practices of these churches are based on shamanistic knowledge about the use of plants, and the traditional use of ayahuasca was reserved for experts. Elements of Christianity and spiritist traditions such as Kardecismo were incorporated into the worship and beliefs of these churches.

Two plants are used in religious activity. The first is the ayahuasca species of *Banisteriopsis* and the second is chacruna (*Psychotria viridis*), the latter of which has dimethyltryptamine, which places it on a scheduled list throughout the world. The UDV was founded in the early 1960s by José Gabriel da Costa, who learned to use ayahuasca from the rubber-gathering populations along the Brazilian borders between Bolivia and Peru. We can say that these religious organizations throughout history have been characterized as struggling for differentiation.

Over time there was a shift from the personal, small-scale, individually organized sessions that characterized mestizo use in Peru and Bolivia that I described in my research to an organization that is institutionalized in Brazil, such as the UDV. Moreover, since the 1980s, there are also religious and nonreligious ayahuasca-using groups in both rural and urban zones that are influenced by the New Age movement and draw upon the phenomenon of the new religious consciousness. Environmental concerns, in addition to spirituality, are included in the ideology of these groups. Followers in urban areas are generally middle-class civil servants, psychotherapists, small entrepreneurs, military personnel, and intellectuals. There is a real feeling that middle-class people are searching for spiritual development or self-knowledge as well as drug addicts who are in need of treatment with ayahuasca—an increasing trend since the end of the 1990s. With the sacramental use of ayahuasca in the UDV, and its spiritually motivated approach, this has been an effective basis for legitimization and social control.

I was fortunate to work with the UDV starting in the 1990s, culminating in 2005 with the publication of our team's research, shortly before the church won a case in the United States Supreme Court that allowed them to continue to use ayahuasca as a sacrament in their religious rituals. In 2000 we assembled a multinational team to investigate the psychosocial and neurocognitive influences of ayahuasca on a group of youth who took it every month, and a matched control group of non-users, in three Brazilian cities—São Paulo, Campinas, and Brasilia. I helped edit and contributed to an issue of the *Journal of Psychoactive Drugs* to report on our findings and to include other scholars' work on ayahuasca. As Charles Grob, my coeditor, and I pointed out, when managed, hallucinogenic-induced altered states of consciousness occur under optimal conditions, there are salutary outcomes. The use of ayahuasca as a sacrament attempts to offer spiritual, emotional, and ethical support to those who ingest the tea. As people drink it, they became part of a religious congregation and a religious event that has as its major goal the development of spirituality in its adherents. People who drink the tea participate as family units and adolescents are included.

An earlier study by Dr. Grob and his colleagues showed that members of the UDV had high levels of functioning compared to normal controls. This included healthier personality measures and superior neuropsychological functioning. The church provided a protective and supportive community.

The history of the UDV is quite interesting. During the course of the mestizo use of ayahuasca, many rubber gatherers in the late nineteenth and early twentieth centuries had access to this plant and its rituals. One person, Mestre Gabriel (a.k.a. José Gabriel da Costa), who founded the UDV in 1961 in Porto Velho, Rondônia, in Brazil, incorporated *hoasca* (the Portuguese word for ayahuasca) into the church rituals. Elements of Christianity, spiritualism (widespread in Latin America throughout the nineteenth century), and influences from the mestre's experience with other Afro-Brazilian religions all coalesced. This is called syncretization in anthropology—the blending of religious elements that we see as a process in most belief systems throughout the world.

The UDV church is organized into a hierarchical structure comprised of a master board, a council board, and instructive member boards. Followers are arranged according to their level of spiritual development, called degree. The oral transmission of beliefs plays an important role in the church, and the ritual experience of ingesting hoasca serves as a teaching vehicle for adherents. As a syncretic religion, the UDV has elements of shamanism, Christianity, and spiritism. Shamanism values the altered state of consciousness as a means to control and dominate spirit forces in nature. Many people have access to such altered states of consciousness, and the hoasca potion enables members of the UDV to achieve an experience akin to this shamanic experience. Curing plays a less prominent part in the ritual activity of the UDV, somewhat different from the native shamanic tradition.

Our research with UDV adolescents and a matched control group took a long time to complete, with many researchers and specialists involved in assessing the long-term effects on cognitive functioning. According to the laws of the UDV, the use of ayahuasca is restricted to religious ceremonies in which multigenerational families meet twice a month for four hours. The adolescents are encouraged to join their parents and drink ayahuasca tea during the ceremonies. Adherents commonly believe that ayahuasca is harmless and potentially beneficial for adolescents, as long as it is imbibed in a religious context.

Currently in Brazil, adolescent membership in the UDV is estimated at more than 1,200. Eighty-four adolescents voluntarily participated in our study and were randomly selected from among congregants at three different UDV churches. The control group also consisted of randomly selected teens who attended similar schools as those the research subjects attended. Two groups of UDV adolescents between the ages of fifteen and nineteen, of both sexes, comprised the study group. The teens had drunk ayahuasca within a ritual context at least twenty-four times during the last two years prior to the testing. The average age was sixteen-and-a-half, and most of them were white. Their educational level ranged from first-year high school to first-year college. The second group, the control, had forty adolescents who had never drunk ayahuasca. They were matched on sex, age, race, and educational level.

Subjects were recruited from various public and private schools.

A comprehensive battery of neuropsychological tests was given to all the teenagers to assess their overall level of cognitive functioning. These tests, administered in Portuguese, assessed attention, concentration, intelligence, language, memory, executive functioning, processing speed, and visuomotor skills. (The technical data was made available in the June 2005 issue of the *Journal of Psychoactive Drugs*.) This was the first study to focus on the cognition of long-term ayahuasca-using adolescents.

The primary finding of the study was that there was no overall difference in neuropsychological performance between the group of ayahuasca-consuming adolescents and the group that had never used the substance. Both groups performed well and presented similar results in most measures. The researchers found no evidence of ill effects from ayahuasca ingestion on the young people who participated with their families in ceremonial rituals using psychoactive substances. Because the UDV adolescents use much less alcohol, marijuana, and other intoxicants that do have a negative influence on cognition, the question arises as to whether ayahuasca may actually protect the UDV adolescents from further harm.

Qualitative Study of Ayahuasca

In addition to the neuropsychological batteries of tests given to both groups, we decided to have a qualitative component as well. When I was in Brazil in 1997, I observed focus groups conducted by my colleagues that included young people. These groups included individuals who used ayahuasca and those who did not. At that time, we decided to develop moral and ethical vignettes for the qualitative aspect of the study, as well as a long questionnaire about the social characteristics of the adolescents. The vignettes were designed to measure moral and ethical considerations of the UDV and control teens. In contemporary society, drug and alcohol use is often associated with excessive risk taking, impulsivity, and a disregard for safety and consequences. We believed that the vignettes would permit an honest self-reporting by teens of their potential responses to situations that posed conflict and would register their general level of maturity.

Overall, there were few if any differences in responses between the UDV adolescents and the controls. Friends of the UDV teens were drawn from church members and less from schoolmates compared to control teens. Unlike the controls, the UDV youth were less confrontational, they found clandestine premarital sex to be distasteful, and they were thrifty, responsible, and concerned about the welfare of others. They had a better quality of home life when compared to their counterparts. They exhibited greater optimism than controls. The qualitative data is quite revealing of the fact that the teenagers appear to be healthy, thoughtful, considerate, and bonded to their families and religious peers.

HALLUCINOGENS AND REDEMPTION

The practice of drug substitution refers to the use of one substance to obviate and negate the cravings for and withdrawal from a second. Methadone, in lieu of heroin, is perhaps the best known example.

After my work with the União do Vegetal Church in Brazil, it became clear to me that drug substitution was at work among a fairly large number of members of their church. Many had given up lives that had once included cocaine, alcohol, tobacco, opiates, and other recreational drugs for a life of rectitude and dedication. Now the only psychedelic they ingested was ayahuasca, always in a ritual context, twice a month. This model of redemption argues that the proper use of one psychoactive substance within a spiritual or clinical environment can help to free a person from the adverse effects of their addiction to another substance and in this way the person is restored as a functioning member within his community. Our research in Brazil showed how a person who is now an active member of the church was able to abstain from addictive substances such as alcohol and opiates. I interviewed eleven mestres in Manaus and understood that almost all of them had once led lives of violence and antisocial behavior before joining the UDV. In these examples we see the concept of suggestibility hard at work.

Today, throughout the world, a variety of both natural and synthetic substances are used as drug substitutes. Of particular interest are the hallucinogens (which themselves are not addictive). In recent decades, we see the use of these substances as substitutes for addictive drugs like heroin, alcohol, methamphetamines, and so on. The hallucinogens that are most frequently used for these purposes include ayahuasca (*Banisteriopsis caapi*), which is usually mixed with chacruna (*Psychotria viridis*); iboga (*Tabernanthe iboga*); LSD (a semisynthetic derivative of the fungus *Claviceps purpurea*); and peyote (*Lophophora williamsii*).

Methadone is effective because it binds to the same receptor sites as heroin (and morphine and codeine), thereby blocking the cell's ability to respond to these opiates. It is also intensely addictive in itself, thus not always successful in transforming a person's psychosocial functioning. In contrast, other types of substances that may be substituted for drugs that are damaging to a person are efficacious because they produce changes in more global psychosocial functioning; in this way they aid the addicted person in assessing and altering negative, self-destructive patterns of behavior, thus helping him avoid using those drugs that have caused him harm in the first place.

Historically, many of these hallucinogenic substances have been used in formal religious contexts. Studies of both the historical and contemporary use of hallucinogens have suggested that the states they induce can have profoundly positive, even life-changing effects on people, not the least because they often provide insights into the meanings of psychological dilemmas. Because these substances can produce an awesome range of experiences that encompass those of diverse religious traditions, it is only natural that their effects have often been interpreted in religious terms.

One of the most important concepts that has been developed to explain the process by which a troubled person can be (re)integrated into his community is that of redemption. The use of this term has allowed researchers to focus on the metaphoric, and not the specific religious and historical, use of the term, as referring to personal redemption. It appears that one substance, through a combination of neurophysiological and psychocultural factors, can effect the distancing of a person from the use of another drug. This, in turn, can lead to the person readopting attitudes and behaviors that are more acceptable to her social group, and a reintegration—redemption—within that particular milieu.

The search for meaning is an important variable in human affairs. People in Western society can be motivated to forego the damaging drug and to strive for meaning to enhance their lives. It is interesting to see the direction in which drug substitution is occurring today. As research in this area continues, we note how different cultures, both modern and traditional, have recognized the universal importance of the hallucinogenic-aided redemptive process in reintegrating wayward people into a harmonious relationship with their community.

13

Psychedelics
and Drug Tourism

AN UGLY DIMENSION OF AMAZONIAN psychedelic use is the runaway drug tourism that is occurring, in which unsuspecting visitors from the United States and Europe are lured by mostly unscrupulous men and women into purchasing mysticism in the Amazon. One of my articles calls on social scientists to take responsibility, however inadvertently they may have contributed to this phenomenon and its dangers and casualties, both psychiatric and physical. This gives rise to a public-health dilemma of wide proportions. Finally, I summarize my recent book on drug tourism, coauthored by my colleague Roger Rumrrill, and I present interviews with twenty-seven ayahusaca healers, including neoshamans found in Amazonian aboriginal societies, among rural and urban mestizos, and even foreigners who take over and try to conduct healing sessions when they have no training or knowledge of drug interactions.

MEA CULPA:
DRUG TOURISM AND
THE ANTHROPOLOGIST'S RESPONSIBILITY

I first wrote about drug tourism in 1994 to describe charlatans who toured visitors from the First World though the Peruvian, Brazilian, and Ecuadorian Amazon so they could participate in plant-hallucinogenic sessions with ayahuasca. This phenomenon, which is a dark side of globalization, has increased in the past fifteen years and has caused serious yet poorly documented health hazards for the clients of these neoshamans.

"Commercial" shamanism in Peru has become a system in which foreigners are given a powerful plant psychedelic at a cost of $300 to $500 a visit. This compares to the $20 to $30 cost for local people. Drug rituals as commercial undertakings can generate a sizable income from the tourists involved. Government authorities have not curtailed this activity and seem to look the other way, despite international treaties that concern the drug interdiction of DMT, a substance contained in one of the ayahuasca additives, chacruna. The DMT that is contained within it is a Schedule 1 drug whose use is prohibited by the Controlled Substances Act of 1970.

In several publications over the past few years, I have pointed out that anthropologists inadvertently have played a major role in diffusing esoteric knowledge to the general public as they study and analyze traditional psychedelic rituals in their writings and professional talks. Despite the fact that many, myself included, have published in peer-reviewed journals and academic settings, or have presented papers in professional conferences and avoided sensationalizing findings, this is not enough. The work of scholars has been disseminated to what Spanish philosopher Ortega y Gasset has, in his 1929 book *The Revolt of the Masses,* called the "democratic masses."

Anthropologists have a responsibility to pay attention to the differences between new religions' sacramental use of plant hallucinogens such as what we see in the União do Vegetal Church in Brazil and the trendy hallucinogenic experiences of urban educated men and women who tour Latin America simply to get high. From an ethical and relativistic perspective, this drug tourism is harmful to those who participate in it. It changes and effectively destroys traditional urban and rural hallucinogenic healing traditions, which have their roots in prehistory.

The neoshamans are basically businessmen who fleece unsuspecting visitors. Some of these so-called healers develop rituals and procedures that are a burlesque of what they believe an altered state should be. Some use mud baths and nudity in their group healing rituals, which is totally dissimilar to anything I saw while attending traditional ayahuasca rituals in the 1960s and 1970s.

These "healers" do not screen tourists for prior illnesses or health conditions. Most of them have never been apprentices, nor have they fasted or adhered to special diets, which traditional healers do to enhance their ability to understand the plant's hallucinogenic effects. The neoshamans are predominantly mestizo middle-class men and women hoping to get rich quick. In many ways they usurp the traditional role of folk healers or curanderos, and in so doing they contribute to the ongoing demise of a cultural healing system by diluting its methods and intention.

Many of the neoshamans lack the experience, appropriate personality, and requisite training for this work. Many, if not most, are unable to accurately diagnose the illnesses, both physical and psychological, that their tourist-clients suffer from, thus they are unable to treat their clients with any measure of success. Nor do they have knowledge about chemical interactions. For example, the combination of ayahuasca and antibiotics can cause poisoning. There are scores of foods and drinks that interact poorly with ayahuasca. Sometimes the drug tourist's condition worsens, and the client has to be rescued or sometimes even hospitalized. On occasion, madness or death has followed, as when one of these neoshamans adds nightshade plants to the ayahuasca mixture.

Roger Rumrrill and I, in our book *A Hallucinogenic Tea Laced with Controversy,* interviewed twenty-seven neoshamans. We summarized our data on these people, who are mostly men (80 percent). Their ages ranged from forty to sixty, with a few older people. Most had no formal or professional training and had not been influenced by Western medicine. They focused mainly on psychosomatic disorders. A majority of them had learned their trade from family members and friends who practice folk medicine. None were involved in mystical organizations (e.g., the Rosicrucians) nor admitted to accepting the existence of witch-craft beliefs that are still widespread in the community. All of them used ayahuasca as well as other plants, including toé and chiricsanango.

As far as they were concerned, their clients faced little or no danger from the use of ayahuasca. They denied that their clients reported any problems. These healers are mostly enterpreneurs who travel around the world by invitation to major cities. Many maintain their own personal Web page, or their center's. They edit brochures and some manage tourism firms. There is a shamanic service in Peruvian Amazon cities in which local ayahuasqueros are contracted to provide shamanic sessions. The neoshamans do not cure because they have a calling, like don Hilde, but rather as a way to make a fast buck.

Drug tourism cries out for regulation: these psychedelic chemicals are potent. The neoshamans' lack of understanding about them is frightening to contemplate. These people are unlike traditional mestizo or indigenous healers who use the plant, who work within a ritualized context and learn about the plant through periods of long and rigorous apprenticeship. The drug tourism that we see in contemporary Peru and the Amazon region is merely a footnote to drug trafficking around the world.

A HALLUCINOGENIC TEA
LACED WITH CONTROVERSY

What is a sacrament in one country is an illicit drug in another. This hallucinogenic brew, ayahuasca, made from a meandering vine native to the Amazonian rain forest, has been taken as a religious sacrament across several cultures in South America. Spiritual leaders, shamans, and their followers consider the tea and its main component, *Banisteriopsis caapi*, to be enlightening and healing, hence the translation of *ayahuasca:* "vine of the spirits."

Ayahuasca has come to the United States. As a result, there have been legal battles that have gone as high as the U.S. Supreme Court. The Brazilian church União do Vegetal, with a branch in Santa Fe, New Mexico, uses the hallucinogen in its ceremonies as a sacrament, much the same way Roman Catholics use wine in the Eucharist. The UDV has fought for governmental approval to do so and received a favorable outcome in February 2006. In *A Hallucinogenic Tea Laced with Controversy,* Roger Rumrrill and I documented the use of ayahuasca by tribal societies of the Amazon and described the phenomenon of drug tourism in detail, looking at the neoshamans—some good, some bad, some terrible. Accounts from tourists from the United States and Europe are also presented. The neoshamans are unable to treat their problems, and so the tourists often worsen, and many suffer from deep psychological traumas. The diverse approaches of the UDV before the Supreme Court are also examined in the book, as well as the weakness of the U.S. government's case against ayahuasca as a sacrament in the church. Finally, the future of ayahuasca and its globalization issues give us pause to reflect on the failure of the War on Drugs, specifically as it pertains to psychedelics.

Epilogue

WHAT KIND OF STUDENT OF psychedelics am I? I recognize that we truly use only a small percentage of our sensoria. Unlike writers such as the late Terence McKenna, I don't embrace astrology, psychoanalytic theory, or mythic figures who communicate with contemporary human beings. I'm not so sure about interspecies communication or alien abductions either. My credo has always been Talmudic in nature, as I see the search for knowledge as a spiritual enterprise. It really feels good to know things and to respect diverse belief systems and to try to suppress one's deeply socialized ethnocentrism. My journey has been and will continue to be a search for information on these magical plants and how they have contributed to human survival.

I have been working with two journals, the *Anthropology of Consciousness,* published by a section of the American Anthropological Association, and the *Journal of Psychoactive Drugs,* which has published many of my articles over the years. Our hope is to set up a feature of the *Anthropology of Consciousness* for a call for shamanic voices to be published in future issues, many of which I expect will deal with plant psychedelics and wisdom traditions of the world. The guardians of memory and the stewards of wisdom traditions deserve a voice, a voice from which we can all learn. This brings to mind an old *Peanuts* comic strip in which Lucy asks Linus what he is going to do when he grows up. He says he's going to go to the university. Lucy excitedly replies that it is wonderful that he would use such knowledge to help people. But Linus says that he is just nosy.

The psychedelics fit in nicely here. We may wish to apply newly acquired wisdom to our own self-understanding, an understanding of the world we live in, and the lived worlds of others. Or we may wish to apply that knowledge to the betterment of humankind. For some of us, knowing in itself is sacred. For others it is merely a tool to participate in self-understanding, while still others are engaged in a focus on the need for social and cultural change and to learn from these traditions.

Cultivating empathy in order to discover the life quests of others is a noble goal. We need to explore the multifarious symbolic universes that we create or are born into. We need to provide opportunities for critical reflection on our own cultural roots and that of others. I have always maintained that my work with psychedelics and my personal experiences, however limited, have enabled me to feel comfortable when I work with people in the throes of spiritual emergencies.

There is a real need for the countervailing presence of these wisdom traditions, in light of the tremendous and powerful negative influences of the commercialization of all human values regnant in the world today. Others will want to seek light and see with clarity a transformation out of the negative elements in their personality, to reach a state of sincere, intimate communication with the self, others, and even the divine. The traditions presented in this memoir and its research findings are perhaps a step in this direction.

Glossary

aliado: a spirit ally of healers or witches.

anquilostoma: hookworm illness.

ayahuasca: various species of the *Banisteriopsis* vine; used in healing in the Amazon.

barriada: a slum settlement.

brujo/bruja: a witch who takes money to harm a person's enemies.

Bwiti cult: a cult that uses the psychedelic *Tabernanthe iboga* in West African religious rituals.

chonta: a thorn introduced by a witch into a person's body to cause illness.

gringa: a white woman, European or American.

hoasca: a Portuguese word for ayahuasca.

mapacho: *Nicotiana rustica* tobacco used along with plant psychedelics in Salas and Belen.

mesa: a ritual table for sacred and magical items, used in San Pedro healing ceremonies on the north coast of Peru.

Pachacama: Inca sun god.

pituri: *Duboisia hopwoodii,* a plant psychedelic used by Australian Aborigines until the early part of the twentieth century.

pusanga: a love potion that causes a person to fall in love with the perpetrator.

ribereño: a farmer living along one of the many river systems in the Peruvian Amazon.

San Pedro: *Trichocereus pachanoi* cactus containing mescaline and used in northern coastal folk healing in Peru.

saladera: a culturally specific illness believed to result from evil maneuvers of people who use salt to cause their enemies bad luck.

schacapa: a bunch of leaves held together by a cord and used as a percussion instrument in ayahuasca sessions.

Septrionismo de la Amazonía: a mystical religious order that don Hilde belonged to in Pucallpa, Peru.

tambo: a temporary wall-less shelter found in northern coastal Peru, used in San Pedro healing rituals.

tanrillo: a small domesticated bird, the leg of which is used to cast love-magic spells.

teonanácatl: an Aztec term for *stropharia* and *psilocybe* hallucinogenic mushrooms.

União do Vegetal: Brazilian church using ayahuasca as a sacrament in its rituals.

velorio: a wake held for a deceased person.

vidente: a healer believed to be a prophet with gifts of telepathy.

Viracocha: an Inca god with a large clergy.

wilka: DMT-containing snuff used by the Incas.

yaravec: Inca court orator.

Published Works of
Marlene Dobkin de Rios, Ph.D.

www.marlenedobkinderios.com

BOOKS: SOLE AUTHOR

Visionary Vine: Hallucinogenic Healing in the Peruvian Amazon. San Francisco: Chandler Publishing Co., 1972. Reprinted by Waveland Press, Prospect Heights, Ill., 1984.

Hallucinogens: Cross-cultural Perspectives. Albuquerque: University of New Mexico Press, 1984.

Amazon Healer: The Life and Times of an Urban Shaman. Bridport, England: Prism Press, 1992.

BOOKS: COAUTHOR

Dobkin de Rios, Marlene, and Oscar Janiger. *LSD, Spirituality, and the Creative Process.* Rochester, Vt.: Park Street Press, 2003.

Dobkin de Rios, Marlene, and Roger Rumrrill. *A Hallucinogenic Tea Laced with Controversy: Ayahuasca in the Amazon and the U.S.* Westport, Conn.: Praeger Publishing Co., 2008.

ARTICLES: SOLE AUTHOR

"*Trichocereus pachanoi:* A Mescaline Cactus Used in Folk Healing in Peru." *Economic Botany* 22, no. 2 (1968): 191–94.

"Folk Curing with a Psychoactive Cactus in N. Peru." *International Journal of Social Psychiatry* 15, no. 1 (1968–1969): 23–56.

"Curanderismo Psicodélico en el Perú: Continuidad y Cambio." *Mesa Redonda de Ciéncias Prehistóricas y Antropológicas.* Lima. Catholic University of Peru

(1969) 92–96. Reprinted in *Psiquiatría Folklórico,* edited by Carlos Alberto Seguin. 235–240, Lima. Ediciones Edmar, l979.

"La cultura de la pobreza y la mágia de amor: Un síndrome urbano en la selva Perúana." *America indígena* 29, no. 3 (1969): 3–16.

"Fortune's Malice: Divination, Psychotherapy, and Folk Medicine in Peru." *Journal of American Folklore* 82, no. 324 (1969): 38–41. Reprinted in *Américas* (Washington, D.C.: Organization of American States, 1981): 109–14.

"*Banisteriopsis* used in Witchcraft and Folk Healing in Iquitos, Peru." *Economic Botany* 24, no. 35 (1970): 296–300.

"A Note on the Use of Ayahuasca among Mestizo Populations in the Peruvian Amazon." *American Anthropologist* 72, no. 6 (1970): 1419–22.

"Ayahuasca, the Healing Vine." *International Journal of Social Psychiatry* 17, no. 4 (1971): 256–69.

"Curanderismo con la soga alucinógena (ayahuasca) en la selva Perúana." *America indígena* 31, no. 3 (1971): 37–76.

"The Anthropology of Drug-Induced Altered States of Consciousness: Some Theoretical Considerations." *Sociologus* 22, no. 1 (1972): 147–51.

"Hallucinogenic Therapeutics among a Civilized Indian Population in the Peruvian Amazon." *International Mental Health Research Newsletter* 14, no. 1 (1972): 1–6.

"The Non-Western Use of Hallucinogenic Agents." *Drug Use in America: Problem in Perspective,* appendix, vol. 1. Second Report of the U.S. National Commission on Marihuana and Drug Abuse (Washington, D.C.: U.S. Govt. Printing Office, 1972): 1143–1289.

"The Use of Hallucinogenic Substances in Peruvian Amazonian Folk Healing." Unpublished Ph.D. dissertation. University of California, Riverside, 1972.

"Curing with Ayahuasca in a Peruvian Amazon Slum." *Hallucinogens and Shamanism,* edited by Michael J. Harner (New York: Oxford University Press, 1973): 67–86.

"Peruvian Hallucinogenic Folk Healing: An Overview." *Psychiatry: Proceedings of the 5th World Congress of Psychiatry,* vol. 2, edited by Ramond de la Fuente and Maxwell Weisman (New York: Excerpta Medica 1973): 1189–98.

"Cultural Persona in Drug-Induced Altered States of Consciousness." *Social and Cultural Identity: Problems of Persistance and Change,* edited by Thomas Fitzgerald. Southern Anthropology Society Proceedings, no. 8 (Athens, Ga.: University of Georgia Press, 1974): 17–24.

"The Influence of Psychotropic Flora and Fauna on Maya Religion." *Current Anthropology* 15, no. 2 (1974): 147–64.

"San Pedro." *Narcotic Plants of the New World Indians: An Anthology of Texts from the 16th Century to the Present,* edited by Hedwig Schleiffer. (New York: Mac-Millan Publishing Co., 1974): 338–45.

"A Visionary Vine from the Peruvian Amazon." *Bulletin,* University of Pennsylvania Morris Arboretum 25, no. 1 (1974): 3–4.

"Man, Culture and Hallucinogens: An Overview." *Cannabis and Culture,* edited by Vera Rubin (The Hague: Mouton Publishers, 1975).

"The Maya and the Water Lily." *New Scholar* 2 (1975): 299–308.

"Plant Hallucinogens and Power in the Pre-Colombian Art of Ancient Peru." *Altered States of Consciousness and Mental Health.* Edited by Colleen Ward (New York: Sage Publishing Co., 1975): 285–300.

"Los alucinógenos de origen vegetal y las pampas de Nazca." Arqueologica PUC, *Boletin del Seminario de Arqueologia,* no. 17–18, publication no. 106 (1975–76): 99–100.

"The Wilderness of Mind: Sacred Plants in Cross-cultural Perspective." Sage Research Papers in the Social Sciences, Cross-cultural Series no. 90–039, 1976. Monograph.

"The Relationship between Witchcraft Beliefs and Psychosomatic Illness." *Anthropology and Mental Health,* edited by Joseph Westermeyer (The Hague: Mouton Publishers, 1976): 11–18.

"Una teoría transcultural del uso de los alucinógenos de origen vegetal." *Etnofarmacología de plantas alucinógenas Latinoamericas,* edited by José L. Diaz, 224–31, Cuadernos Científicos 4. Centro Mexicano de Estudios en Farmacodependéncia. Reprinted in *América indígena* 37, no. 2 (1976): 191–304.

"Hallocinogenic Ritual as Theatre." *Journal of Psychoactive Drugs* 9, no. 3 (1977): 265–68.

"Plant Hallucinogens, Out of Body Experiences and New World Monumental Earthworks." *Drugs, Rituals and Altered States of Consciouness.* Edited by Brian du Toit (Amsterdam: Baklma Press, 1977): 237–49.

"Plant Hallucinogens and the Religion of the Mochica—an Ancient Peruvian Peoples." *Economic Botany* 31, no. 2 (1977): 189–203.

"The Maya and the Water Lily." *The New Scholar* 5, no. 2 (1978): 299–307.

"La cultura de la pobreza y el amor mágico: Un síndrome urbano en la selva Perúana." *Psiquiatria folklorica,* edited by Carlos Alberto Seguin (Lima: Ediciones Edmar, 1979): 67–72.

"Mexican Migrant Tubercular Patients' Attitudes Concerning Alcohol." *Journal of Psychoactive Drugs* 11, no. 4, (1979): 347–51.

"La relacion entre las creéncias en la brujeria y le enfermedad psicosomática." *Salud y nutricion en la selva Perúana,* edited by Alberto Chirif (Lima: Centro de Estudios Amazonicos): 1979.

"Socio-Economic Characteristics of an Amazon Urban Healer's Clientele." *Social Science and Medicine* 15B, (1981): 51–63.

"Plant Hallucinogens, Sexuality and Shamanism in the Ceramic Art of Ancient Peru." *Journal of Psychoactive Drugs* 14 (1982): 77–80.

"Religion und pflanzehnhallüzinogene im Prakolumbischën Peru—Moche und Nazca." *Rausch und realitat: Drögen im Kulturvergleich*, vol. 1 (Cologne: Rautenstrauch-Joest Museams fur Vokerkünde, 1982): 457–66.

"The Vidente Phenomenon in Third World Traditional Healing: An Amazonian Example." *Medical Anthropology* 8, no. 1 (1984): 60–70.

"Saladera: A Culture-Bound Misfortune Syndrome in the Peruvian Amazon." *Culture, Medicine, and Psychiatry* 5 (1981): 193–213. Reprinted in *The Culture-Bound Syndromes: Folk Illness of Psychiatric and Anthropological Interest*, edited by Ronald C. Simons and Charles C. Hughes (Dordrecht: Reidel Publishing Co., 1985): 215–23.

"Curacíon urbana Amazónica: Concordancia o discrepancia doctrinal?" *Amazonia Perúana* 6 (1989): 11–18.

"A Modern-Day Shamanistic Healer in the Peruvian Amazon: Pharmacopoeia and Trance." *Journal of Psychoactive Drugs* 21, no. 1 (1989): 91–100.

"Plant Hallucinogens and Power in the Pre-Colombian Art of Ancient Peru." *Altered States of Consciousness and Mental Health,* edited by Colleen Ward (New York: Sage Publishing Co., 1989): 443–50.

"A Response to Lucas's 'Entheology.'" *Journal of Psychoactive Drugs* 27, no. 3(1992): 277–78.

"Twenty-Five Years of Hallucinogenic Studies in Cross-cultural Perspective." *Newsletter, Anthropology of Consciousness,* American Anthropological Association 4, no. 1 (1993): 1–8.

"Halluzinogene im kulturvergleich." *Welten des bewusstseins*, vol. 1. Edited by Adolf Dittrich, Albert Hofmann, and Hanscarl Leuner (Berlin: Verlag fur Wissenschaft und Bildung, 1993): 45–67.

"Drug Tourism in the Amazon." *Newsletter, Society for the Anthropology of Consciousness* 5, no. 1 (Washington, D.C., 1994): 16–19.

"What We Can Learn from Shamanic Healing: Brief Psychotherapy with Latino Immigrant Clients." *American Journal of Public Health* 92, no. 10 (2002): 1576–78.

"Interview with Guillermo Arrevalo, a Shipibo Urban Shaman, by Roger Rumrrill." *Journal of Psychoactive Drugs* 37, no. 2 (2005): 193–202.

"Anthropoloist as Fortuneteller." *Skeptic Magazine* 12, no. 4 (2007): 44–49.

BOOK REVIEWS,
BRIEF COMMUNICATIONS, AND ABSTRACTS

Abstract: "Ayahuasca, the Healing Vine." *Transcultural Psychiatric Research Review* 7 (1970): 186–88.

Review: Manual Córdova-Rios. "Wizard of the Upper Amazon." *American Anthropologist* 74, no. 6 (1970): 1423–24; also in *Medical Anthropology Newsletter* 3 no. 3 (1972): 5–6.

Review: Francisco Guerra. "The Pre-Colombian Mind: A Study into the Aberrant Nature of Sexual Drives, Drugs Affecting Behaviour, and the Attitude towards Life and Death, with a Survey of Psychotherapy in Pre-Columbian America." *Medical Anthropology Newsletter* 4, no. 1 (1972): 7–8.

Review: G. Reichel-Dolmatoff. "The Shaman and the Jaguar: A Study of Narcotic Drugs among the Indians of Colombia." *Medical Anthropology Newsletter* 6 (1975): 7–8.

Abstract: "Cultural Persona in Drug-Induced Altered States of Consciousness." *Transcultural Psychiatric Research Review* 13 (1975): 18–19.

Review: Vera Rubin and Lambros Comitas. "Ganja in Jamaica: A Medical Anthropological Study of Chronic Marihuana Use." *L'Homme* 16, no. 4 (1976): 149–53.

Review: Thomas Szasz. "Ceremonial Chemistry: The Ritual Persecution of Drugs, Addicts, and Pushers." *Medical Anthropology Quarterly* 7, no. 2 (1976): 12–13.

Comment on "The Cult of the Serpent in the Americas." *Current Anthropology* 18, no. 3 (1977): 429–57.

Review: José Gushiken. "Tuno, el curandero." *Américas* (1980): 72.

Review: Gerardo Reichel-Dolmatoff. "Beyond the Milky Way: Hallucinatory Imagery of the Tukano Indians." *Américas* (1981): 57–63.

Review: Peter K. Levison, et al., eds. "Commonalities in Substance Abuse and Habitual Behavior." *Journal of Psychoactive Drugs* 16, no. 3 (1984): 269–70.

Review: Pamela Watson. "This Precious Foliage: A Study of the Aboriginal Psychoactive Drug Pituri." *Journal of Psychoactive Drugs* 16, no. 4 (1984): 367–68.

Review: Johannes Wilbert. "Tobacco and Shamanism in South America." *Medical Anthropology Quarterly* 3, no. 1 (1989): 7.

First Word: "Drug Tourism in the Amazon." *OMNI Magazine* (1994): 6.

Rejoinder: "The Bad Trip Revisited." *Newsletter, Society for the Anthropology of Consciousness* 16, no. 1 (1994): 45–47.

Abstract: "Historical and Cross-cultural Perspectives on the Use of Hallucinogens in Spiritual Practice." *Problems of Drug Dependence 2001: Proceedings of the 63rd Annual Scientific Meeting*. Edited by Louis Harris, 182. U.S. Dept. of Health and Human Services, National Institutes of Health, The College on Problems of Drug Dependence, Inc. (2002): 119–20.

Review: "Ecstasy: In and About Altered States." *Journal of Nervous and Mental Disease* 195, no. 8 (2007): 710.

JOINT PUBLICATIONS

Katz, Fred, and Marlene Dobkin de Rios. "Hallucinogenic Music: An Analysis of the Role of Whistling in Peruvian Ayahuasca Healing Sessions." *Journal of American Folklore* 84, no. 333 (1971): 320–27.

Rios, Oscar, and Marlene Dobkin de Rios. "Psychotherapy with Ayahuasca (a Harmine Drink) in Northern Peru: Research Report and Proposal." *Transcultural Psychiatric Research Review* 4 (1971): 162–64.

Katz, Fred, and Marlene Dobkin de Rios. Abstract: "Hallucinogenic Music." *Transcultural Psychiatric Research Review* 9 (1972): 149–50.

Janiger, Oscar, and Marlene Dobkin de Rios. "Suggestive Hallucinogenic Properties of Tobacco." *Medical Anthropology Newsletter* 4, no. 4 (1973): 6–11.

Dobkin de Rios, Marlene, and Fred Katz. "Some Relationships between Music and Hallucinogenic Ritual: The Jungle Gym in Consciousness." *Ethos* 3, no. 1 (1975): 64–76.

Janiger, Oscar, and Marlene Dobkin de Rios. "Nicotiana an Hallucinogen?" *Economic Botany* 30, no. 2 (1976): 149–51.

Dobkin de Rios, Marlene, and David E. Smith. "The Function of Drug Rituals in Human Society: Continuities and Changes." *Journal of Psychoactive Drugs* 9, no. 3 (1977): 269–76.

———. "Drug Use and Abuse in Cross-cultural Perspective." *Human Organization* 36, no. 1 (1977): 14–21. Reprinted in *Culture and Psychopathology*. Edited by J. Mezzich (New York: Columbia University Press, 1984): 278–86.

Smith, David, Donald Wesson, John Kramer, and Marlene Dobkin de Rios, eds. "Drugs, History and Culture." *Journal of Psychoactive Drugs* 9, no. 3 (1977)

Dobkin de Rios, Marlene, and Mercedes Cárdenas. "Plant Hallucinogens, Shamanism, and Nazca Ceramics." *Journal of Ethnopharmacology* 2 (1980): 233–46.

Emboden, William, and Marlene Dobkin de Rios. "Narcotic Ritual Use of Water Lilies among Ancient Egyptian and Maya." *Folk Healing and Herbal Medicine*. Edited by George Meyer and Kenneth Blum (Springfield, Ill.: Charles Thomas Publishers, 1981): 275–86.

Martinez, Suzanne, Bruce Achauer, and Marlene Dobkin de Rios. "Ketamine Use in a Southern California Burn Center: Hallucinogen or Debridement Facilitator?" *Journal of Psychoactive Drugs* 17, no. 1 (1985): 45–50.

Dobkin de Rios, Marlene, and Michael Winkelman. "Shamanism and Altered

States of Consciousness: An Introduction." *Journal of Psychoactive Drugs* 21, no. 1 (1989): 1–8.

———, eds. "Trance and Shamanism." *Journal of Psychoactive Drugs* 21, no. 1 (1989): 1–6.

Winkelman, Michael, and Marlene Dobkin de Rios. "Psychoactive Properties of !Kung Bushmen Medicine Plants." *Journal of Psychoactive Drugs* 21, no. 1 (1989): 51–60.

Dobkin de Rios, Marlene, and Charles S. Grob. "Hallucinogens, Suggestibility, and Adolescence in a Cross-cultural Perspective." *Yearbook for Ethnomedicine and the Study of Consciousness* 3 (1992): 113–32.

Grob, Charles S., and Marlene Dobkin de Rios. "Adolescent Drug Use in Cross-cultural Perspective." *Journal of Drug Issues* 22, no. 1 (1992): 121–38.

Dobkin de Rios, Marlene, Charles S. Grob, and John Baker. "Hallucinogens and Redemption." *Journal of Psychoactive Drugs* 34, no. 3 (2002): 239–48.

Dobkin de Rios, Marlene, and Charles S. Grob. "Interview with Jeffrey Bronfman, Representative Mestre for the União do Vegetal Church in the United States." *Journal of Psychoactive Drugs* 37, no. 2 (2005): 189–92.

Dobkin de Rios, Marlene, Charles S. Grob, Enriquez Lopez, et al. "Ayahuasca in Adolescence: Qualitative Results." *Journal of Psychoactive Drugs* 37, no. 2 (2005): 135–40.

Dobkin de Rios, Marlene, and Charles S. Grob, eds. "Ayahuasca Use in Cross-cultural Perspective." *Journal of Psychoactive Drugs* 37, no. 2 (2005): 1–4.

Doering-Silveira, Evelyn, Enrique Lopez, Charles S. Grob, and Marlene Dobkin de Rios. "Ayahuasca in Adolescence: A Neuropsychological Assessment." *Journal of Psychoactive Drugs* 37, no. 2 (2005): 123–28.

Doering-Silveira, Evelyn, Charles S. Grob, and Marlene Dobkin de Rios. "Report on Psychoactive Drug Use among Adolescents Using Ayahuasca within a Religious Context." *Journal of Psychoactive Drugs* 37, no. 2 (2005): 141–44.

Silveira, Dartieu, Charles S. Grob, and Marlene Dobkin de Rios. "Ayahuasca in Adolescence: A Preliminary Psychiatric Assessment." *Journal of Psychoactive Drugs* 37, no. 2 (2005): 129–34.

Groisman, Alberto, and Marlene Dobkin de Rios. "Ayahuasca, the U.S. Supreme Court, and the UDV–U.S. Government Case: Culture, Religion, and Implications of a Legal Dispute." *Psychedelic Medicine,* vol. 1. Edited by Michael J. Winkelman and Thomas Roberts (Westport, Conn.: Praeger, 2007): 251–70.

Bibliography

Balandier, George. *Ambiguous Africa: Cultures in Collision*. Paris: Plon, 1959.

Castaneda, Carlos. *Teachings of Don Juan*. Los Angeles: University of California Press, 1968.

Cushman, Phillip. "Why the Self Is Empty: Toward a Historically Situated Psychology." *American Psychology* 45, no. 5 (1990): 599–611.

Diaz, José. "Etnofarmacologia de algunos psicotrópicos vegetales de México." *Etnofarmacologia de plantas alucinógenas Latinoamericanas*. Edited by J. L. Diaz (Mexico City: Centro Mexicano de Estudios en Farmacodependencia–CEMEF, 1976): 278–89.

Ekman, Paul. *Emotions Revealed*. New York: Henry Holt and Co., 2003.

Fernandez, James W. *Bwiti: An Ethnography of the Religious Imagination in Africa*. Princeton: Princeton University Press, 1982.

Frecska, Ede, et al. "Effects of Ayahuasca on Binocular Rivalry with Dichoptic Stimulus Alternation." *Psychopharmacology* 173 (2003): 79–87.

Gehricke, Jean, et al. "Smoking to Self-Medicate Attentional and Emotional Dysfunctions." *Nicotine and Tobacco Research* 9 no. 4 (2007): 523–36.

Grob, Charles S., et al. "Human Psychopharmacology of Hoasca, a Plant Hallucinogen Used in Ritual Context in Brazil." *Journal of Nervous and Mental Disease* 184, no. 2 (1994): 86–94.

Grof, Stanislav. "Theoretical and Empirical Base of Transpersonal Psychology and Psychotherapy: Observations from LSD Research." *Journal of Transpersonal Psychology* 4 (1972): 45–80.

Johnston, Thomas F. "Datura Use in a Tsonga Girls' Puberty School." *Economic Botany* 26, no. 4 (1972): 340–51.

Rappaport, Roy. "Ritual, Sanctity, and Cybernetics." *American Anthropologist* 73, no. 1 (1971): 59–76.

Reay, Maria. "Mushroom Madness in the New Guinea Highlands." *Oceania* 31:3 (1960): 137–39.

Siskind, Janet. "Visions and Cures among the Sharanahua." *Hallucinogens and Shamanism*. Edited by M. J. Harner. New York: Oxford University Press, 1973.

Tart, Charles, ed. *Altered States of Consciousness*. New York: Wiley, 1969.

Wasson, R. Gordon, et al. *The Road to Eleusis: Unveiling the Secret of the Mysteries*. Los Angeles: Hermes Press, 1997.

Winkelman, M. *Shamanism: The Neural Ecology of Consciousness and Healing* Greenwich, Conn.: Greenwood Publishing Group, 2000.

Index

BOOKS OF RELATED INTEREST

LSD, Spirituality, and the Creative Process
Based on the Groundbreaking Research of Oscar Janiger, M.D.
by Marlene Dobkin de Rios, Ph.D., and Oscar Janiger, M.D.

Plants of the Gods
Their Sacred, Healing, and Hallucinogenic Powers
by Richard Evans Schultes, Albert Hofmann, and Christian Rätsch

The Encyclopedia of Psychoactive Plants
Ethnopharmacology and Its Applications
by Christian Rätsch

DMT: The Spirit Molecule
A Doctor's Revolutionary Research into the
Biology of Near-Death and Mystical Experiences
by Rick Strassman, M.D.

Inner Paths to Outer Space
Journeys to Alien Worlds through Psychedelics
and Other Spiritual Technologies
*by Rick Strassman, M.D., Slawek Wojtowicz, M.D.,
Luis Eduardo Luna, Ph.D., and Ede Frecska, M.D.*

LSD: Doorway to the Numinous
The Groundbreaking Psychedelic Research into
Realms of the Human Unconscious
by Stanislav Grof, M.D.

Tryptamine Palace
5-MeO-DMT and the *Bufo alvarius* Toad
by James Oroc

The Jaguar that Roams the Mind
An Amazonian Plant Spirit Odyssey
by Robert Tindall

INNER TRADITIONS • BEAR & COMPANY
P.O. Box 388, Rochester, VT 05767
1-800-246-8648
www.InnerTraditions.com
Or contact your local bookseller